HOW TO UNDERTAKE HANDYMAN PROJECTS

The Ultimate DIY Guide for Beginners: Mastering Simple Repairs, Home Maintenance Hacks, and Easy Renovation Projects

The Fix It Guy

Table of Contents

Introduction

Hey there, fellow DIY enthusiast! Are you tired of constantly shelling out your hard-earned cash for simple home repairs and improvements? Do you find yourself daydreaming about tackling those nagging projects around the house, but feel intimidated by the thought of wielding a hammer or drilling into walls? Well, fear not! You're about to embark on a thrilling journey that will transform you from a hesitant novice to a confident, capable handyman.

In "How to Undertake Handyman Projects," we'll demystify the world of DIY and equip you with the knowledge and skills necessary to conquer a wide range of home maintenance tasks, repairs, and weekend improvements. No longer will you be at the mercy of expensive contractors or the whims of a landlord. With this book as your trusty guide, you'll develop the prowess to handle most common household issues with ease, saving you time, money, and the headache of waiting for someone else to do the job.

But the benefits of becoming a DIY handyman extend far beyond financial savings. As you tackle each project, you'll feel a profound sense of accomplishment and pride in your work. Your home will become a reflection of your skills and dedication, and you'll gain a deeper appreciation for the intricacies of the structures and systems that surround you daily. Plus, you'll impress your friends and family with your newfound abilities, and perhaps even inspire them to join you on your DIY adventures.

Now, before you start envisioning yourself as the next Bob Vila, let's take a moment to assess your current skills and comfort level. Whether you're a complete beginner who's never touched a screwdriver, or you've dabbled in minor repairs but yearn to take on more complex projects, this book meets you where you are.

We'll start with the basics and gradually build your confidence and expertise, ensuring that you have a solid foundation before diving into more advanced tasks.

Of course, no handyman is complete without a reliable set of tools. But don't worry – you won't need to break the bank or fill your garage with expensive, specialized equipment. In the coming pages, we'll guide you through the essential tools every handyman should have in their arsenal, focusing on versatile, high-quality items that will serve you well for years to come. With a modest investment in the right tools, you'll be prepared to tackle a vast array of projects with confidence and efficiency.

So, are you ready to unleash your inner handyman and transform your home, one project at a time? If you're nodding your head with enthusiasm, then let's dive in! Together, we'll demystify the world of DIY, empowering you to take control of your home's maintenance and improvements. Get ready to roll up your sleeves, grab your tools, and experience the unparalleled satisfaction of a job well done. Your journey to becoming a master handyman starts now!

Chapter 1
Basic Home Maintenance
Unclogging Drains and Toilets

As a homeowner or renter, one of the most common and frustrating issues you'll encounter is a clogged drain or toilet. These blockages can quickly disrupt your daily routine and cause unpleasant odors or even water damage if left untreated. Fortunately, with a few simple tools and techniques, you can often resolve these problems without the need for a costly plumber.

1. Identifying the Problem:

Before attempting to unclog a drain or toilet, it's essential to assess the severity of the blockage. Slow-draining sinks, tubs, or showers indicate a partial blockage, while a completely stopped drain or a toilet that won't flush suggests a more significant issue. Take note of any unusual odors or sounds coming from the drain, as these can help pinpoint the location and nature of the clog.

2. Gathering Your Tools:

To tackle most drain and toilet clogs, you'll need a few basic tools:
- Plunger: A plunger is the most common tool for unclogging drains and toilets. Ensure you have a cup plunger for sinks and a flange plunger for toilets.
- Drain Snake or Auger: For more stubborn clogs, a drain snake or auger can help break through the blockage.
- Protective Gloves: Always wear gloves to protect your hands from bacteria and harsh cleaning agents.
- Bucket: Keep a bucket nearby to catch any water or debris that may come out of the drain.

3. Plunging Techniques:

a. Sinks, Tubs, and Showers:

- Remove the drain cover or stopper, and place the plunger directly over the drain opening.
- Ensure there's enough water in the sink, tub, or shower to cover the plunger's head.
- Begin plunging vigorously, using an up-and-down motion to create suction and pressure.
- Continue plunging for 20-30 seconds, then check if the water drains freely.
- Repeat the process if necessary.

b. Toilets:

- If the toilet bowl is full, remove some water using a bucket until the water level is about halfway up the bowl.
- Place the flange plunger over the toilet bowl's opening, ensuring a tight seal.
- Plunge vigorously, maintaining the seal, for 20-30 seconds.
- Flush the toilet to see if the clog has been removed. If the water level rises, be prepared to turn off the water supply to prevent overflow.
- Repeat the plunging process if needed.

4. Using a Drain Snake or Auger:

If plunging doesn't resolve the clog, a drain snake or auger can help break through the blockage.

- Insert the end of the snake or auger into the drain opening.
- Rotate the handle clockwise while pushing the cable through the drain pipe.
- When you feel resistance, continue turning the handle to allow the auger head to break through the clog.
- Once the clog has been penetrated, retract the snake or auger by rotating the handle counterclockwise.
- Run hot water through the drain for a few minutes to flush away any remaining debris.

8

5. Preventive Maintenance:

To minimize the occurrence of clogs, adopt these preventive measures:

- Avoid flushing non-biodegradable items, such as wipes, paper towels, or feminine hygiene products.
- Use drain covers or strainers to catch hair, food particles, and other debris.
- Regularly pour boiling water or a mixture of baking soda and vinegar down drains to help clear away buildup.
- Schedule periodic professional drain cleaning to maintain the health of your plumbing system.

By mastering the art of unclogging drains and toilets, you'll save time and money while ensuring the smooth function of your home's plumbing. Remember, if you encounter a particularly stubborn clog or suspect a more serious issue, don't hesitate to contact a professional plumber to protect your home from potential water damage.

Fixing Leaky Faucets and Showerheads

Leaky faucets and showerheads are not only annoying but can also waste a significant amount of water, leading to higher utility bills and potential damage to your home. Fortunately, most leaks can be fixed with a few basic tools and a little know-how. In this section, we'll guide you through the process of diagnosing and repairing common types of leaky faucets and showerheads.

1. Identifying the Type of Faucet:

Before attempting to fix a leaky faucet, it's crucial to determine the type of faucet you have, as repair methods vary. The most common types include:

- Compression Faucets: These have separate handles for hot and cold water and use rubber washers to control water flow.
- Cartridge Faucets: These have a single handle that controls both temperature and water flow using a cartridge.
- Ceramic Disk Faucets: These also have a single handle but use ceramic discs to control water flow.
- Ball Faucets: These have a single handle that moves over a ball-shaped cap to control water flow and temperature.

2. Gathering Your Tools:

To repair a leaky faucet or showerhead, you'll need the following tools:

- Adjustable Wrench
- Pliers
- Flathead and Phillips Screwdrivers
- Replacement Parts (depending on the type of faucet)
- Plumber's Grease or Teflon Tape
- Cloth or Bucket (to catch any water)

3. Fixing a Compression Faucet:

a. Preparation:
- Turn off the water supply to the faucet by closing the shutoff valves under the sink.
- Remove the decorative handles by unscrewing the screws or prying off the caps.
- Unscrew the packing nut using an adjustable wrench.

b. Replacing the Washer:
- Remove the stem assembly from the faucet body.
- Inspect the rubber washer at the bottom of the stem. If it's worn or damaged, replace it with a new one of the same size.
- Reassemble the stem and reattach the packing nut and handles.

c. Testing:
- Turn the water supply back on and test the faucet for leaks.
- If the leak persists, repeat the process, ensuring all parts are properly seated and tightened.

4. Fixing a Cartridge, Ceramic Disc, or Ball Faucet:

a. Preparation:
- Turn off the water supply to the faucet.
- Remove the handle by unscrewing any visible screws or prying off the cap.

b. Accessing the Cartridge, Disc, or Ball:
- For cartridge faucets, pull out the cartridge using pliers.
- For ceramic disc faucets, remove the disc cylinder by unscrewing the retaining nut.
- For ball faucets, remove the cap and ball assembly.

c. Replacing the Cartridge, Disc, or Ball:
- Inspect the removed part for signs of wear or damage. If necessary, replace it with a new one specific to your faucet model.
- Clean the faucet body and reassemble the parts, applying plumber's grease to the new parts for a smooth operation.

d. Testing:
- Turn the water supply back on and test the faucet for leaks.
- If the leak persists, double-check that all parts are correctly installed and properly aligned.

5. Fixing a Leaky Showerhead:
a. Preparation:
- Remove the showerhead from the shower arm using an adjustable wrench.
- Inspect the threads on the shower arm and showerhead for any debris or mineral buildup.

b. Cleaning and Replacing the Washer:
- Clean the threads and remove any old plumber's tape or debris.
- Replace the rubber washer inside the showerhead if it's worn or damaged.

c. Reassembling and Testing:
- Wrap the shower arm threads with new plumber's tape, ensuring a tight seal.
- Reattach the showerhead to the shower arm and tighten it securely with an adjustable wrench.
- Turn on the water and test the showerhead for leaks. If leaks persist, tighten the connection further or replace the showerhead.

By following these steps, you can successfully fix most leaky faucets and showerheads, saving water and money in the process. Remember to refer to your specific faucet model's instructions if you encounter any unique challenges, and don't hesitate to call a plumber if you're unsure about any part of the repair process.

Repairing Drywall Holes and Cracks

Drywall, also known as gypsum board or sheetrock, is a common material used for interior walls and ceilings. Over time, drywall can develop holes, cracks, or dents due to various factors such as accidental impacts, settling of the house, or wear and tear. Repairing these imperfections is a crucial skill for any DIY enthusiast, as it helps maintain the appearance and integrity of your walls. In this section, we'll cover the steps to repair different types of drywall damage.

1. Assessing the Damage:
   Before beginning any repair, evaluate the extent of the damage to determine the best course of action.
   - Small Holes (less than 1/2 inch): These can be easily filled with spackling compound.
   - Medium Holes (1/2 to 3 inches): These require a patch made of drywall or mesh tape.
   - Large Holes (larger than 3 inches): These necessitate a more involved repair using a drywall patch.
   - Cracks: Depending on the size and depth, cracks can be repaired using drywall tape and joint compound.

2. Gathering Your Tools and Materials:
   To repair drywall holes and cracks, you'll need the following supplies:
   - Drywall Saw or Utility Knife
   - Joint Compound (also known as drywall mud)
   - Drywall Tape (paper or mesh)
   - Drywall Patches (for larger holes)
   - Sandpaper (120-grit and 150-grit)
   - Putty Knife or Drywall Knife (4-inch and 6-inch)
   - Spackle or Lightweight Spackling Compound (for small holes)
   - Paint and Paintbrush (to match the existing wall color)

3. Repairing Small Holes:

a. Cleaning the Area:
- Remove any loose debris from the hole using a utility knife or sandpaper.

b. Filling the Hole:
- Apply a small amount of spackle or lightweight spackling compound to the hole using a putty knife.
- Smooth the spackle flush with the surrounding wall, and allow it to dry completely (refer to the product's instructions for drying times).

c. Sanding and Painting:
- Once dry, sand the repaired area with 120-grit sandpaper until smooth and flush with the wall.
- Wipe away any dust with a damp cloth and apply touch-up paint to blend the repair with the surrounding wall.

4. Repairing Medium Holes:

a. Cutting a Patch:
- Cut a piece of drywall or mesh tape slightly larger than the hole.

b. Attaching the Patch:
- Apply a thin layer of joint compound around the hole's edges.
- Place the patch over the hole and press it firmly into the joint compound.
- Apply another layer of joint compound over the patch, feathering the edges to blend with the surrounding wall.
- Allow the joint compound to dry completely.

c. Sanding and Painting:
- Sand the repaired area with 120-grit sandpaper, followed by 150-grit for a smoother finish.
- Wipe away dust and apply touch-up paint to match the wall color.

5. Repairing Large Holes:

a. Cutting the Damaged Area:
- Using a drywall saw, cut a square or rectangular shape around the damaged area, ensuring to expose the wall studs on either side.

b. Attaching Blocking:
- Cut a piece of scrap wood to fit between the exposed studs.
- Attach the blocking to the studs using drywall screws.

c. Cutting and Attaching the Patch:
- Cut a piece of drywall to fit the hole, using the blocking as a backing.
- Secure the patch to the blocking with drywall screws.

d. Taping and Mudding:
- Apply drywall tape to the seams between the patch and the surrounding wall.
- Cover the tape with a thin layer of joint compound, feathering the edges.
- Allow the first coat to dry, then apply a second and third coat, sanding between each coat with 120-grit sandpaper.

e. Final Sanding and Painting:
- Sand the final coat with 150-grit sandpaper until smooth.
- Wipe away dust and apply touch-up paint to blend the repair with the wall.

6. Repairing Cracks:

a. Widening the Crack:
- Using a utility knife, slightly widen the crack to create a small trench for the joint compound.

b. Applying Tape and Mud:
- Apply drywall tape over the crack, centering it over the trench.
- Cover the tape with a thin layer of joint compound, feathering the edges.

- Allow the first coat to dry, then apply a second and third coat, sanding between each coat with 120-grit sandpaper.

c. Final Sanding and Painting:

- Sand the final coat with 150-grit sandpaper until smooth.
- Wipe away dust and apply touch-up paint to blend the repair with the wall.

By following these steps, you can effectively repair various types of drywall holes and cracks, restoring the smooth, seamless appearance of your walls. With practice and patience, you'll develop the skills necessary to tackle any drywall repair project with confidence.

Maintaining HVAC Systems

A well-maintained heating, ventilation, and air conditioning (HVAC) system is essential for ensuring a comfortable and healthy living environment while also optimizing energy efficiency and prolonging the life of your equipment. Regular maintenance can help prevent costly repairs and breakdowns, ultimately saving you money in the long run. In this section, we'll discuss the key steps in maintaining your HVAC system.

1. Understanding Your HVAC System:

Before diving into maintenance tasks, it's crucial to understand the basic components of your HVAC system and how they function.

a. Heating:
- Furnaces (gas, oil, or electric) heat air, which is then distributed throughout your home via ductwork.
- Heat pumps (air-source or ground-source) transfer heat from one place to another, providing both heating and cooling.

b. Ventilation:
- Ductwork distributes conditioned air throughout your home.
- Ventilation systems (such as exhaust fans) remove stale air and moisture from your home.

c. Air Conditioning:
- Central air conditioners cool and dehumidify the air, which is then circulated through the ductwork.
- Ductless mini-split systems provide targeted cooling to individual rooms or zones.

2. Changing Air Filters:

One of the simplest and most important maintenance tasks is regularly replacing your HVAC system's air filters.

a. Locating Filters:
- Filters are typically located in the return air grille or the blower compartment of your furnace or air handler.

b. Choosing the Right Filter:
- Select a filter with the appropriate size and MERV (Minimum Efficiency Reporting Value) rating for your system.
- Higher MERV ratings provide better filtration but may restrict airflow if too high for your system.

c. Replacement Schedule:
- Change filters every 1-3 months, depending on usage, household conditions, and manufacturer recommendations.
- More frequent changes may be necessary for households with pets, allergies, or heavy HVAC usage.

3. Cleaning and Inspecting Components:

Regular cleaning and inspection of HVAC components can help maintain efficiency and identify potential issues before they escalate.

a. Outdoor Unit (AC or Heat Pump):
- Remove debris, such as leaves or grass clippings, from the unit and surrounding area.
- Gently clean the fins with a soft-bristled brush or fin comb to remove dirt and straighten bent fins.
- Ensure proper airflow by maintaining a 2-foot clearance around the unit.

b. Indoor Unit (Furnace or Air Handler):
- Vacuum the blower compartment and burners (for gas furnaces) to remove dust and debris.
- Inspect the drain pan and condensate lines for clogs or leaks, and clean as necessary.
- Check the flame sensor and pilot light (for gas furnaces) for proper operation.

c. Ductwork:
- Check for visible leaks, gaps, or loose connections in the ductwork.
- Consider professional duct cleaning every 3-5 years, or as needed based on household conditions.

4. Programmable Thermostats:

Installing and properly using a programmable thermostat can significantly improve your HVAC system's efficiency and comfort levels.

a. Installation:

- Choose a thermostat compatible with your HVAC system (e.g., conventional, heat pump, or multi-stage).
- Follow the manufacturer's wiring and installation instructions carefully.

b. Programming:

- Set temperature schedules based on your daily routines and occupancy patterns.
- Adjust settings for seasonal changes and vacation periods to optimize energy savings.

c. Regular Battery Replacement:

- Replace batteries annually or as indicated by the low battery warning to maintain proper operation.

5. Professional Maintenance:

While many maintenance tasks can be performed by homeowners, it's essential to schedule professional HVAC maintenance at least once a year.

a. Timing:

- Schedule heating system maintenance in the fall, before the heating season begins.
- Schedule cooling system maintenance in the spring, before the cooling season starts.

b. Technician Tasks:

- Inspect and test all system components for proper operation and safety.
- Clean and lubricate moving parts, such as motors and bearings.
- Measure refrigerant levels and check for leaks (for air conditioners and heat pumps).

- Test and calibrate thermostats and other controls.
- Identify and address any potential issues or areas for improvement.

By following these maintenance guidelines and staying proactive about the care of your HVAC system, you can ensure optimal performance, energy efficiency, and longevity. Regular maintenance not only provides peace of mind but also helps create a more comfortable and healthier living environment for you and your family.

Cleaning Gutters and Downspouts

Maintaining clean and functional gutters and downspouts is crucial for protecting your home from water damage, as they play a vital role in directing rainwater and snowmelt away from your home's foundation, walls, and roof. Clogged or damaged gutters can lead to various issues, such as basement flooding, soil erosion, and even structural damage. In this section, we'll walk through the steps to properly clean and maintain your gutters and downspouts.

1. Safety First:
   Before beginning any gutter cleaning project, prioritize safety to avoid accidents and injuries.
   a. Sturdy Ladder:
   - Use a stable, well-maintained ladder that extends at least three feet above the gutter.
   - Place the ladder on a firm, level surface and avoid resting it against the gutters.
   b. Protective Gear:
   - Wear non-slip shoes or boots with good traction.
   - Use work gloves to protect your hands from sharp debris and prevent cuts.
   - Consider wearing safety goggles to shield your eyes from dirt and debris.
   c. Buddy System:
   - If possible, work with a partner who can hold the ladder steady and assist in case of an emergency.

2. Removing Debris:
   The first step in cleaning gutters is to remove accumulated debris, such as leaves, twigs, and dirt.
   a. Manual Removal:
   - Using a gutter scoop or your gloved hands, carefully remove debris from the gutters, starting at the downspout and working your way towards the opposite end.

- Place the debris in a bucket or drop it onto a tarp on the ground for easy cleanup.

b. Wet/Dry Vacuum:
- For gutters with smaller debris or hard-to-reach areas, a wet/dry vacuum with a gutter cleaning attachment can be an efficient solution.

c. Gutter Cleaning Tools:
- Consider using specialized gutter cleaning tools, such as telescoping wands or gutter robots, to minimize the need for ladder work.

3. Flushing the Gutters:
After removing the bulk of the debris, flush the gutters to ensure they're clear and free-flowing.

a. Garden Hose:
- Using a garden hose with a nozzle attachment, start at the end opposite the downspout and flush the gutters, directing water towards the downspout.
- Check for any leaks, holes, or sagging areas that may require repairs.

b. Downspout Cleaning:
- If water isn't flowing freely through the downspout, there may be a clog.
- Insert the hose into the downspout and turn on the water to force out any blockages.
- If the clog persists, use a plumber's snake or a long-handled brush to remove the obstruction.

4. Inspecting and Repairing:
While cleaning the gutters, take the opportunity to inspect them for any damage or issues that need to be addressed.

a. Leaks and Holes:
- Check for any signs of leaks or holes in the gutters or downspouts.

- Small holes can be repaired using gutter sealant or patches, while larger holes may require section replacement.

b. Sagging Gutters:
- Look for any sagging or pulling away from the fascia board.
- Tighten or replace loose gutter hangers to ensure proper pitch and drainage.

c. Rust and Corrosion:
- Inspect for signs of rust or corrosion, particularly on older metal gutters.
- Remove rust with a wire brush and apply a rust-inhibiting paint to prevent further damage.

5. Regular Maintenance:

To keep your gutters and downspouts functioning optimally, regular maintenance is essential.

a. Cleaning Frequency:
- Clean gutters at least twice a year, typically in the spring and fall.
- Adjust the frequency based on your location and the surrounding tree coverage.

b. Gutter Guards:
- Consider installing gutter guards or covers to minimize debris accumulation and reduce cleaning frequency.
- Choose a type that suits your specific needs and budget, such as mesh screens, reverse curves, or micro-mesh guards.

c. Trimming Trees:
- Trim overhanging tree branches to reduce the amount of debris falling into the gutters.
- Maintain a safe distance between trees and your home's roofline to prevent damage.

By following these steps and maintaining a regular cleaning schedule, you can ensure that your gutters and downspouts remain in good condition, effectively protecting your home from water damage and other associated issues. If you're uncomfortable with heights or lack the necessary tools, consider hiring a professional gutter cleaning service to handle the task safely and efficiently.

Chapter 2
Electrical Repairs and Upgrades

Understanding Electrical Safety

Electricity is a powerful and potentially dangerous force that should be approached with caution and respect. Before attempting any electrical repairs or upgrades, it is crucial to understand the fundamental principles of electrical safety to protect yourself, your family, and your home from the risks associated with electrical work. In this section, we'll discuss the key aspects of electrical safety and best practices to follow when working with electricity.

1. Electrical Hazards:

Electricity poses several hazards that can result in serious injury, property damage, or even death.

a. Electric Shock:

- Electric shock occurs when an individual comes into contact with live electrical components or wiring.
- The severity of the shock depends on factors such as voltage, current, duration of contact, and the body's resistance.
- Symptoms can range from a mild tingling sensation to severe burns, cardiac arrest, or death.

b. Electrical Fires:

- Electrical fires can be caused by overloaded circuits, faulty wiring, or malfunctioning appliances.
- These fires can spread quickly and cause significant property damage if not addressed promptly.

c. Arc Flash:

- An arc flash is a sudden release of energy caused by an electrical arc, resulting in intense heat, light, and pressure.
- Arc flashes can cause severe burns, hearing damage, and impact injuries.

2. Personal Protective Equipment (PPE):

When working with electricity, wearing appropriate PPE is essential to minimize the risk of injury.

a. Insulated Gloves:
- Wear rubber insulating gloves rated for the voltage level you'll be working with.
- Inspect gloves for any holes, tears, or damage before each use.

b. Safety Glasses or Face Shield:
- Protect your eyes from potential sparks, debris, or arc flashes.
- Choose safety glasses with side shields or a full-face shield for optimal protection.

c. Flame-Resistant Clothing:
- Wear clothing made from flame-resistant materials, such as treated cotton or Nomex.
- Avoid synthetic materials that can melt or ignite easily.

d. Non-Conductive Footwear:
- Wear shoes with insulating soles, such as rubber or dielectric footwear.
- Avoid shoes with metal components or conductive materials.

3. Lockout/Tagout Procedures:

Lockout/Tagout (LOTO) procedures are crucial for preventing accidental energization of electrical systems during maintenance or repairs.

a. De-energize Equipment:
- Turn off the power supply to the equipment or circuit you'll be working on.
- Verify that the equipment is de-energized using a voltage tester or multimeter.

b. Lockout Devices:
- Apply a physical lockout device, such as a padlock, to the power source to prevent others from inadvertently turning it back on.

- If multiple people are working on the same equipment, each person should apply their own lock.

c. Tagout Labels:

- Attach a prominent tagout label to the locked-out device, indicating the reason for the lockout, the name of the person who applied it, and the date.
- Tagout labels serve as a visual warning to others not to remove the lockout device or re-energize the equipment.

4. Electrical Tools and Equipment:

Using the right tools and equipment is essential for safe and effective electrical work.

a. Insulated Tools:

- Use tools with insulated handles, such as pliers, wire strippers, and screwdrivers, to reduce the risk of electric shock.
- Inspect tools regularly for any damage or wear to the insulation.

b. Grounded or Double-Insulated Tools:

- Choose power tools that are either grounded (three-prong plug) or double-insulated to minimize the risk of electrical shock.
- Double-insulated tools have a special insulation system that protects the user even if the tool develops an internal fault.

c. Ground Fault Circuit Interrupters (GFCIs):

- Use GFCIs when working with electrical equipment in damp or wet locations.
- GFCIs detect ground faults and quickly shut off the power to prevent electric shock.

5. Electrical Codes and Standards:

Electrical work must comply with national, state, and local electrical codes and standards to ensure safety and consistency.

a. National Electrical Code (NEC):
- The NEC is a comprehensive set of guidelines for electrical design, installation, and inspection in the United States.
- Familiarize yourself with the relevant NEC sections for the type of electrical work you'll be performing.

b. Local Building Codes:
- Check with your local building department for any additional codes or requirements specific to your area.
- Obtain necessary permits and arrange for inspections as required by local regulations.

c. Professional Assistance:
- If you're unsure about any aspect of electrical work or encounter a situation beyond your skill level, consult a licensed electrician.
- Attempting complex electrical repairs or upgrades without proper knowledge and experience can result in serious safety hazards.

By understanding and adhering to these electrical safety principles, you can minimize the risks associated with electrical work and ensure a safer environment for yourself and others. Always prioritize safety, use appropriate PPE, follow LOTO procedures, and comply with relevant codes and standards. Remember, if you have any doubts or concerns, it's always best to seek the assistance of a qualified professional.

Replacing Light Fixtures and Switches

Updating light fixtures and switches is a common home improvement project that can enhance the functionality, efficiency, and aesthetic appeal of your living spaces. Whether you're replacing outdated fixtures or upgrading to more modern, energy-efficient options, the process involves a few key steps to ensure a safe and successful installation. In this section, we'll guide you through the process of replacing light fixtures and switches.

1. Safety First:
   Before beginning any electrical work, always prioritize safety to prevent accidents and injuries.
   a. Turn Off Power:
   • Locate the circuit breaker or fuse box and turn off the power supply to the fixture or switch you'll be replacing.
   • Use a voltage tester to confirm that the power is off before proceeding.
   b. Gather Necessary Tools:
   • Assemble the required tools, such as screwdrivers, wire strippers, pliers, and a voltage tester.
   • Ensure that your tools are insulated and in good condition.
   c. Ladder Safety:
   • If working at heights, use a sturdy ladder that is appropriate for the task.
   • Follow proper ladder safety guidelines, such as maintaining three points of contact and avoiding overreaching.

2. Removing the Old Fixture or Switch:
   The first step in the replacement process is to remove the existing fixture or switch.
   a. Light Fixtures:
   • Remove any shades, bulbs, or covers to access the mounting screws.

- Unscrew and carefully lower the fixture, supporting its weight as you disconnect the wires.
- Take note of the wire connections (hot, neutral, and ground) for reference during installation.

b. Switches:
- Remove the switch cover plate and unscrew the switch from the electrical box.
- Disconnect the wires from the switch terminals, noting their positions (load, line, and ground).

3. Preparing the New Fixture or Switch:

Before installing the new fixture or switch, take the necessary preparatory steps.

a. Compatibility Check:
- Ensure that the new fixture or switch is compatible with your existing electrical system (voltage, wattage, and type of switch).
- Check the manufacturer's instructions for any specific requirements or guidelines.

b. Wire Preparation:
- Use wire strippers to remove about 3/4 inch of insulation from the end of each wire.
- If the wires are frayed or damaged, cut them back to a clean section before stripping.

c. Mounting Considerations:
- For light fixtures, ensure that the mounting bracket is securely attached to the electrical box and can support the weight of the new fixture.
- For switches, verify that the new switch fits properly in the electrical box and aligns with the cover plate.

4. Installing the New Fixture or Switch:
- With the preparation complete, you can now proceed with installing the new fixture or switch.

a. Light Fixtures:
- Connect the fixture wires to the corresponding house wires using wire nuts (hot to hot, neutral to neutral, and ground to ground).
- Carefully tuck the wires into the electrical box and secure the fixture to the mounting bracket.
- Install any shades, bulbs, or covers as directed by the manufacturer.

b. Switches:
- Connect the switch wires to the corresponding house wires (load to one terminal, line to the other, and ground to the green screw or designated ground terminal).
- Carefully tuck the wires into the electrical box and secure the switch using the mounting screws.
- Attach the cover plate and ensure a snug fit.

5. Testing and Finishing Touches:

After installation, it's crucial to test the new fixture or switch to ensure proper operation.

a. Restore Power:
- Turn the power back on at the circuit breaker or fuse box.
- Use a voltage tester to confirm that power is now present at the fixture or switch.

b. Testing:
- For light fixtures, turn on the switch and verify that the fixture illuminates properly.
- For switches, test the functionality by turning the switch on and off and observing the controlled fixture or outlet.

c. Finishing Touches:
- Once you've confirmed proper operation, restore any removed furniture or décor items.
- Clean the fixture or switch cover plate to remove any fingerprints or dust.

- Dispose of the old fixture or switch according to local regulations, recycling when possible.

By following these steps and prioritizing safety throughout the process, you can successfully replace light fixtures and switches in your home. If you encounter any challenges or are unsure about any aspect of the installation, don't hesitate to consult a licensed electrician for assistance.

Remember to always adhere to local building codes and obtain necessary permits for electrical work. Regularly inspecting and maintaining your light fixtures and switches can help ensure their longevity and prevent potential hazards. With updated, energy-efficient fixtures and switches, you can enjoy improved lighting quality, convenience, and potential energy savings in your living spaces.

Installing Ceiling Fans and Dimmer Switches

Ceiling fans and dimmer switches are popular home upgrades that can enhance comfort, energy efficiency, and ambiance in your living spaces. Ceiling fans provide cooling air circulation and can help reduce reliance on air conditioning, while dimmer switches allow you to adjust lighting levels to suit your preferences and create different moods. In this section, we'll walk you through the process of installing ceiling fans and dimmer switches.

1. Choosing the Right Components:
Before beginning the installation, select the appropriate ceiling fan and dimmer switch for your needs.
   a. Ceiling Fans:
   - Consider factors such as room size, ceiling height, blade span, and motor power when selecting a ceiling fan.
   - Choose a fan with the desired style, finish, and features (e.g., light kit, remote control) to complement your room's décor.
   b. Dimmer Switches:
   - Ensure that the dimmer switch is compatible with your lighting type (incandescent, LED, CFL) and wattage.
   - Select a dimmer switch with the desired style, color, and features (e.g., preset levels, remote control).

2. Preparing for Installation:
Proper preparation is key to a successful and safe installation process.
   a. Safety Measures:
   - Turn off the power supply to the relevant circuit at the breaker box.
   - Use a voltage tester to confirm that the power is off before proceeding.

b. Gather Tools and Materials:
- Assemble the necessary tools, such as screwdrivers, wire strippers, pliers, a voltage tester, and a ladder.
- Ensure you have the manufacturer-provided installation hardware and instructions.

c. Mounting Preparation:
- For ceiling fans, check that the electrical box is securely attached to a ceiling joist and rated for the weight of the fan.
- If necessary, install a fan-rated electrical box or brace to provide proper support.

3. Removing Existing Fixtures:

If replacing an existing light fixture or switch, remove them carefully.

a. Light Fixtures:
- Remove any shades, bulbs, or covers to access the mounting screws.
- Unscrew and lower the fixture, supporting its weight while disconnecting the wires.

b. Switches:
- Remove the switch cover plate and unscrew the switch from the electrical box.
- Disconnect the wires from the switch terminals, noting their positions.

4. Installing the Ceiling Fan:

Follow the manufacturer's instructions closely when installing the ceiling fan.

a. Mounting Bracket:
- Attach the mounting bracket to the electrical box, ensuring it is level and secure.

b. Fan Motor Assembly:
- Hang the fan motor assembly onto the mounting bracket, following the provided instructions.

- Make the necessary electrical connections (hot to black, neutral to white, ground to green or bare wire).

c. Blade Installation:
- Attach the fan blades to the blade arms, securing them tightly with the provided screws.
- Attach the blade arms to the fan motor, ensuring they are properly balanced and aligned.

d. Light Kit and Covers:
- If applicable, install the light kit and shades according to the manufacturer's instructions.
- Attach any additional covers or decorative elements as directed.

5. Installing the Dimmer Switch:

Replace the existing switch with the dimmer switch, following the manufacturer's wiring diagram.

a. Wiring Connections:
- Connect the dimmer switch wires to the corresponding house wires (load to one terminal, line to the other, and ground to the green screw or designated ground terminal).
- If necessary, connect any additional wires, such as a neutral wire, as directed by the manufacturer.

b. Mounting and Cover Plate:
- Carefully tuck the wires into the electrical box and secure the dimmer switch using the mounting screws.
- Attach the cover plate and ensure a snug fit.

6. Testing and Final Steps:

After installation, test the ceiling fan and dimmer switch to ensure proper functionality.

a. Restore Power:
- Turn the power back on at the circuit breaker box.
- Use a voltage tester to confirm that power is present at the fan and switch.

b. Testing:

- Turn on the ceiling fan and verify that it rotates smoothly without wobbling or unusual noises.
- Test the fan at various speeds and directions (if applicable) to ensure proper operation.
- Turn on the light kit (if installed) and confirm that it illuminates properly.
- Adjust the dimmer switch through its range to verify smooth dimming control.

c. Final Steps:

- Once you've confirmed proper operation, restore any removed furniture or décor items.
- Clean the fan blades, light fixtures, and dimmer switch cover plate.
- Provide any necessary documentation, such as the manufacturer's warranty and care instructions, to the homeowner.

By following these steps and adhering to the manufacturer's guidelines and local building codes, you can successfully install ceiling fans and dimmer switches in your home. If you encounter any difficulties or are unsure about the installation process, consult a licensed electrician to ensure the work is done safely and correctly.

Regular maintenance, such as cleaning the fan blades, checking for loose connections, and replacing dimmer switches if they malfunction, can help prolong the life of your ceiling fans and dimmer switches. With these upgrades, you can enjoy improved comfort, energy savings, and enhanced control over your home's lighting and ambiance.

Upgrading Electrical Outlets

Electrical outlets are essential components of your home's electrical system, providing convenient access to power for your devices and appliances. Over time, outlets can become outdated, worn, or inadequate for your changing needs. Upgrading your electrical outlets can improve safety, functionality, and convenience. In this section, we'll discuss the process of upgrading electrical outlets and the various types of outlets available.

1. Assessing Your Outlet Needs:
    Before upgrading your outlets, evaluate your specific requirements and the reasons for the upgrade.
  a. Safety Concerns:
  • Replace any outlets that are damaged, cracked, or show signs of wear.
  • Upgrade to GFCI (Ground Fault Circuit Interrupter) outlets in areas prone to moisture, such as kitchens, bathrooms, and outdoor spaces.
  b. Functionality:
  • Consider upgrading to outlets with built-in USB ports for charging devices.
  • Install tamper-resistant outlets to protect children from accidental electric shocks.
  • Upgrade to smart outlets that can be controlled remotely or programmed on a schedule.
  c. Code Compliance:
  • Ensure that your outlet upgrades comply with the latest National Electrical Code (NEC) requirements and local building codes.

2. Types of Electrical Outlets:

There are several types of electrical outlets available, each designed for specific purposes and locations.

a. Standard Outlets:

- These are the most common outlets found in homes, typically providing 15A or 20A of power.
- They have two vertical slots (hot and neutral) and a round or U-shaped ground hole.

b. GFCI Outlets:

- GFCI outlets protect against electric shock by quickly shutting off power when a ground fault is detected.
- They are required in areas prone to moisture, such as kitchens, bathrooms, garages, and outdoor spaces.

c. AFCI Outlets:

- AFCI (Arc Fault Circuit Interrupter) outlets protect against electrical fires caused by arc faults.
- They are required in certain areas, such as bedrooms, living rooms, and hallways, as per the NEC.

d. USB Outlets:

- These outlets have built-in USB ports, allowing you to charge devices without the need for separate adapters.
- They are convenient for locations where charging devices are frequently used, such as bedrooms, offices, and living rooms.

e. Smart Outlets:

- Smart outlets can be controlled remotely using a smartphone app or voice commands.
- They can be programmed to turn on or off on a schedule, monitor energy usage, and integrate with other smart home devices.

3. Preparing for Outlet Upgrades:

Before beginning any outlet upgrades, ensure that you have the necessary tools and follow safety precautions.

a. Safety Measures:

- Always turn off the power to the outlet at the circuit breaker before starting any work.
- Use a voltage tester to confirm that the power is off.
- Wear protective gear, such as gloves and safety glasses.

b. Tools and Materials:

- Gather the required tools, including a screwdriver, wire stripper, voltage tester, and needle-nose pliers.
- Have the new outlets, outlet boxes (if needed), and any additional materials, such as wire connectors and mounting screws.

4. Replacing an Existing Outlet:

Follow these steps to replace an existing outlet with a new one.

a. Remove the Old Outlet:

- Unscrew the outlet cover plate and remove the mounting screws holding the outlet in place.
- Carefully pull the outlet out of the box, taking note of the wire connections.

b. Disconnect the Wires:

- Use a screwdriver to loosen the terminal screws and disconnect the wires from the old outlet.
- If the wires are twisted together, use needle-nose pliers to separate them.

c. Connect the New Outlet:

- Attach the wires to the corresponding terminals on the new outlet (hot to brass screw, neutral to silver screw, ground to green screw).
- Ensure the wires are securely attached and no bare wire is exposed outside the terminals.

d. Secure the New Outlet:
- Carefully tuck the wires back into the outlet box and secure the new outlet with the mounting screws.
- Attach the outlet cover plate and restore power to the circuit.

5. Testing and Safety Considerations:

After upgrading an outlet, it's crucial to test it for proper functionality and ensure safety.

a. Testing the Outlet:
- Use a voltage tester or outlet tester to verify that the outlet is wired correctly and providing power.
- Plug in a device to the outlet to confirm that it operates as expected.

b. GFCI and AFCI Testing:
- For GFCI outlets, press the "test" and "reset" buttons to ensure the outlet trips and resets properly.
- For AFCI outlets, follow the manufacturer's instructions for testing the arc fault protection.

c. Safety Considerations:
- If you're unsure about any aspect of the outlet upgrade process, consult a licensed electrician.
- Regularly inspect your outlets for signs of damage, overheating, or loose connections, and address any issues promptly.

By upgrading your electrical outlets, you can enhance the safety, functionality, and convenience of your home's electrical system. Whether you're replacing old, worn outlets or installing specialized outlets like GFCIs, AFCIs, or USB outlets, following proper procedures and safety precautions is essential.

Remember to comply with the National Electrical Code and local building codes when upgrading outlets, and obtain any necessary permits. If you encounter complex wiring situations or are uncomfortable working with electricity, it's always best to hire a licensed electrician to ensure the work is done safely and correctly.

Troubleshooting Common Electrical Issues

Electrical problems can range from minor inconveniences to serious safety hazards. As a homeowner or DIY enthusiast, it's essential to understand how to troubleshoot common electrical issues safely and effectively. In this section, we'll discuss some of the most common electrical problems and provide step-by-step guidance on how to diagnose and resolve them.

1. Outlets Not Working:

If an outlet stops working, it could be due to various reasons, such as a tripped GFCI, loose connections, or a faulty outlet.

a. Check GFCI Outlets:

- Locate the nearest GFCI outlet (usually in bathrooms, kitchens, or outdoor areas) and press the "reset" button.
- If the GFCI has tripped, it may have shut off power to other outlets on the same circuit.

b. Check Circuit Breakers:

- If resetting the GFCI doesn't resolve the issue, check your main electrical panel for a tripped circuit breaker.
- Turn the tripped breaker fully off and then back on to reset it.

c. Inspect Outlet Connections:

- If the outlet is still not working, turn off the power to the outlet at the circuit breaker and remove the outlet cover plate.
- Check for loose, damaged, or disconnected wires and tighten or reconnect them as needed.

d. Replace Faulty Outlets:

- If the outlet is visibly damaged or if the above steps don't resolve the issue, the outlet may need to be replaced.
- Follow the proper steps for replacing an outlet, as described in the previous section on upgrading electrical outlets.

2. Flickering or Dimming Lights:

Flickering or dimming lights can be caused by various factors, including loose connections, overloaded circuits, or issues with the light fixtures themselves.

a. Check Bulbs and Fixtures:

- Ensure that light bulbs are properly screwed in and are the correct wattage for the fixture.
- Check for loose or damaged light fixtures and tighten or replace them as needed.

b. Inspect Wiring Connections:

- Turn off the power to the affected light fixture at the circuit breaker.
- Remove the light fixture cover and check for loose, damaged, or disconnected wires.
- Tighten or reconnect any loose wires and replace any damaged wires.

c. Assess Circuit Load:

- If the flickering or dimming affects multiple lights or outlets, the circuit may be overloaded.
- Redistribute appliances and devices to other circuits or consider adding a new circuit to alleviate the load.

3. Tripping Circuit Breakers:

Circuit breakers are designed to trip when there's an overload or short circuit to protect your electrical system from damage.

a. Identify the Cause:

- Unplug all appliances and devices connected to the tripped circuit.
- Reset the tripped breaker and plug in the appliances one by one to identify which one is causing the issue.

b. Address Overloaded Circuits:

- If the breaker trips when multiple appliances are in use, the circuit may be overloaded.
- Redistribute appliances to other circuits or consider adding a new circuit to handle the load.

c. Repair Short Circuits:
- If the breaker trips immediately after resetting it, there may be a short circuit in the wiring or an appliance.
- Inspect the wiring and appliances for damage or exposed wires and repair or replace them as needed.

4. Electrical Shocks:
Electrical shocks can be dangerous and indicate a serious problem with your electrical system.
a. Identify the Source:
- If you experience a shock from a specific appliance or outlet, immediately unplug the appliance and stop using the outlet.
b. Check for Wiring Issues:
- Turn off the power to the affected outlet or appliance at the circuit breaker.
- Inspect the wiring for damage, fraying, or exposed wires and repair or replace as needed.
c. Address Moisture:
- If the shock occurred in an area prone to moisture, such as a bathroom or kitchen, ensure that GFCI outlets are installed and functioning properly.
- Repair any leaks or sources of moisture to prevent future shocks.

5. When to Call a Professional:
While some electrical issues can be resolved with basic troubleshooting, certain situations require the expertise of a licensed electrician.
a. Persistent Problems:
- If you've attempted to troubleshoot an issue and it persists or recurs, it's best to consult a professional.
b. Complex Wiring:
- If you encounter complex wiring situations, such as multiple wires connected to a single terminal or wires of unfamiliar colors, consult an electrician.

c. Safety Concerns:
- If you experience frequent electrical shocks, smell burning odors, or notice sparks or smoke coming from outlets or appliances, immediately turn off the power and contact an electrician.

When troubleshooting electrical issues, always prioritize safety. If you're unsure about any aspect of the troubleshooting process or are uncomfortable working with electricity, don't hesitate to seek the assistance of a licensed electrician.

Remember to turn off the power at the circuit breaker before attempting any repairs or inspections, and use proper tools and protective gear. By understanding how to troubleshoot common electrical issues, you can quickly diagnose and resolve minor problems, ensuring the safety and reliability of your home's electrical system.

Chapter 3
Plumbing Projects
Replacing Bathroom and Kitchen Fixtures

Updating bathroom and kitchen fixtures is a great way to improve the functionality, efficiency, and aesthetic appeal of these high-use areas in your home. Whether you're replacing a leaky faucet, upgrading to a water-saving showerhead, or installing a new sink, the process involves a few key steps to ensure a successful and leak-free installation. In this section, we'll guide you through the process of replacing common bathroom and kitchen fixtures.

1. Preparation and Safety:
   Before beginning any plumbing project, it's essential to prepare your work area and prioritize safety.
   a. Turn Off Water Supply:
   • Locate the shut-off valves for the specific fixture you'll be replacing and turn them off completely.
   • If there are no dedicated shut-off valves, turn off the main water supply to the entire house.
   b. Gather Tools and Materials:
   • Assemble the necessary tools, such as adjustable wrenches, pliers, a basin wrench, plumber's tape, and a bucket.
   • Ensure you have the replacement fixture, any required mounting hardware, and new supply lines or fittings.
   c. Protect Your Work Area:
   • Place a protective covering, such as a drop cloth or towels, around the work area to catch any water or debris.
   • Have a bucket or container nearby to collect any residual water from the pipes or fixtures.

2. Removing the Old Fixture:

The first step in replacing a fixture is to remove the existing one carefully.

a. Disconnect Supply Lines:

- Use an adjustable wrench to loosen and disconnect the supply lines from the shut-off valves.
- If the lines are old or corroded, consider replacing them with new, flexible supply lines.

b. Remove Mounting Hardware:

- Locate the mounting nuts or screws that secure the fixture to the countertop, wall, or floor.
- Use a basin wrench or adjustable wrench to loosen and remove the mounting hardware.

c. Lift Out the Old Fixture:

- Carefully lift the old fixture out of its mounting hole or position.
- If the fixture is heavy or awkward, enlist the help of a partner to avoid damage or injury.

3. Preparing for the New Fixture:

Before installing the new fixture, take the time to prepare the area and the new fixture itself.

a. Clean the Mounting Area:

- Remove any old caulk, grime, or debris from the mounting surface using a putty knife or scraper.
- Clean the area thoroughly with a disinfectant to ensure a hygienic and adhering surface for the new fixture.

b. Install Mounting Hardware:

- If the new fixture requires different mounting hardware, install it according to the manufacturer's instructions.
- Ensure that the mounting hardware is securely tightened and properly aligned.

c. Apply Plumber's Tape:
- Wrap plumber's tape (also known as Teflon tape) around the threads of the supply line connections.
- This helps create a watertight seal and prevents leaks at the connection points.

4. Installing the New Fixture:
With the preparation complete, you can now install the new fixture.
a. Position the New Fixture:
- Carefully place the new fixture into the mounting hole or position, ensuring it is properly aligned.
- If necessary, have a partner assist you in holding the fixture steady while you secure it.

b. Secure the Mounting Hardware:
- Use a basin wrench or adjustable wrench to tighten the mounting nuts or screws, following the manufacturer's torque specifications.
- Be careful not to overtighten, as this can damage the fixture or cause cracks in the mounting surface.

c. Connect Supply Lines:
- Attach the supply lines to the shut-off valves and the fixture's water inlets.
- Use an adjustable wrench to tighten the connections securely, ensuring a snug fit.

5. Testing and Finishing Touches:
After installing the new fixture, it's crucial to test it for proper function and leaks.
a. Turn On Water Supply:
- Slowly turn on the shut-off valves or main water supply, allowing the water to flow into the new fixture.
- Check for any leaks at the supply line connections, mounting area, and the fixture itself.

b. Test Functionality:
- Turn on the faucet or showerhead and let the water run for a few minutes.
- Check for proper water flow, temperature control, and drainage.
- If any issues arise, refer to the manufacturer's troubleshooting guidelines or consult a professional plumber.

c. Apply Caulk:
- If necessary, apply a bead of silicone caulk around the base of the fixture to create a watertight seal.
- Smooth the caulk with a wet finger or caulking tool for a neat and professional finish.

d. Clean and Inspect:
- Wipe down the new fixture and the surrounding area to remove any water spots or debris.
- Inspect the installation one final time to ensure everything is secure and properly functioning.

By following these steps and paying attention to the manufacturer's instructions, you can successfully replace bathroom and kitchen fixtures in your home. Remember to prioritize safety, take your time, and double-check your work to prevent leaks and ensure proper functionality.

If you encounter any unexpected issues or feel unsure about any part of the process, don't hesitate to consult a licensed plumber for guidance or professional assistance. With updated, efficient fixtures in place, you can enjoy improved performance, water savings, and a refreshed look in your bathroom and kitchen.

Installing a New Toilet

A toilet is one of the most essential fixtures in any home, and replacing an old or inefficient toilet can improve both the functionality and aesthetics of your bathroom. Whether you're upgrading to a water-saving model or replacing a damaged toilet, the installation process involves several key steps to ensure a proper and leak-free fit. In this section, we'll walk you through the process of installing a new toilet.

1. Preparation and Safety:

Before beginning the installation, ensure you have all the necessary tools and materials and take appropriate safety precautions.

a. Gather Tools and Materials:
- Adjustable wrench, pliers, hacksaw, putty knife, bucket, sponge, and wax ring or rubber seal
- New toilet, bolts, and any additional hardware included with the toilet

b. Turn Off Water Supply:
- Locate the shut-off valve near the base of the toilet and turn it clockwise to shut off the water supply completely
- Flush the toilet to drain the tank and bowl, using a bucket to catch any remaining water

c. Remove Old Toilet:
- Disconnect the water supply line from the shut-off valve using an adjustable wrench
- Remove the tank and bowl separately, unscrewing the bolts that secure them to the floor and carefully lifting them away

2. Preparing the Area:

With the old toilet removed, take the time to clean and prepare the installation area.

a. Remove Old Wax Ring:
- Scrape away the old wax ring from the toilet flange using a putty knife, being careful not to damage the flange
- Clean the flange and surrounding area thoroughly to ensure a proper seal for the new wax ring

b. Inspect Toilet Flange:
- Check the condition of the toilet flange for cracks, damage, or signs of corrosion
- If the flange is damaged, repair or replace it before proceeding with the installation

c. Install New Bolts:
- Insert new bolts into the slots on the toilet flange, ensuring they are properly aligned and secure
- If the bolts are too long, trim them with a hacksaw to the appropriate length

3. Installing the New Toilet:

With the area prepared, you can now install the new toilet.

a. Install Wax Ring or Rubber Seal:
- Place the new wax ring or rubber seal onto the toilet flange, ensuring it is centered and properly seated
- If using a wax ring, be sure to place it with the tapered side facing down towards the flange

b. Position and Secure Bowl:
- Carefully lower the new toilet bowl onto the flange, aligning it with the bolts and pressing it firmly into place
- Place washers and nuts onto the bolts and tighten them alternately to ensure an even seal, being careful not to overtighten

c. Install Tank:
- Place the rubber gasket onto the flush valve opening at the bottom of the tank
- Lower the tank onto the bowl, aligning the bolts with the holes in the tank
- Secure the tank to the bowl using the provided washers and nuts, tightening them alternately for an even fit

4. Connecting and Testing:
With the toilet installed, it's time to connect the water supply and test for proper function and leaks.
a. Connect Water Supply Line:
- Attach the water supply line to the shut-off valve and the fill valve on the toilet tank
- Tighten the connections securely using an adjustable wrench, being careful not to overtighten

b. Turn On Water Supply:
- Slowly turn the shut-off valve counterclockwise to turn the water supply back on
- Check for any leaks at the connections and around the base of the toilet

c. Test Flush and Fill:
- Flush the toilet and observe the tank and bowl for proper filling and draining
- Adjust the water level in the tank if necessary, following the manufacturer's instructions
- If any issues arise, refer to the manufacturer's troubleshooting guide or consult a professional plumber

5. Finishing Touches:
After successfully installing and testing the new toilet, complete the installation with a few finishing touches.
a. Install Toilet Seat:
- Attach the new toilet seat to the bowl according to the manufacturer's instructions

- Ensure the seat is properly aligned and securely fastened

b. Caulk Around Base:
- Apply a bead of silicone caulk around the base of the toilet where it meets the floor
- Smooth the caulk with a wet finger or caulking tool for a neat and finished appearance

c. Clean and Inspect:
- Wipe down the new toilet and surrounding area to remove any debris or water spots
- Inspect the installation one final time to ensure everything is properly connected and functioning

By following these steps and paying close attention to the manufacturer's instructions, you can successfully install a new toilet in your home. Remember to prioritize safety, double-check your work for leaks, and take your time to ensure a proper and secure installation.

If you encounter any unexpected challenges or feel uncertain about any part of the process, don't hesitate to consult a licensed plumber for guidance or professional assistance. With a new, efficiently functioning toilet in place, you can enjoy improved performance, water savings, and an updated look in your bathroom.

Fixing a Running Toilet

A running toilet is a common plumbing issue that can waste a significant amount of water and cause an annoying, constant sound. This problem occurs when water continually flows from the tank into the bowl, even when the toilet hasn't been flushed. In most cases, a running toilet is caused by a faulty or worn-out component in the tank's flushing mechanism. In this section, we'll guide you through the process of diagnosing and fixing a running toilet.

1. Identifying the Cause:
   To fix a running toilet, you first need to determine the cause of the problem. The most common culprits include:
   a. Flapper:
   • The flapper is the rubber seal that covers the flush valve opening at the bottom of the tank.
   • If the flapper is worn, misaligned, or has a damaged chain, it may not seal properly, causing water to leak into the bowl.
   b. Fill Valve:
   • The fill valve controls the water level in the tank and shuts off when the tank is full.
   • If the fill valve is faulty or not properly adjusted, it may cause water to continue running into the tank.
   c. Overflow Tube:
   • The overflow tube prevents the tank from overflowing by directing excess water into the bowl.
   • If the water level in the tank is too high, water will continually flow into the overflow tube and into the bowl.

2. Fixing a Faulty Flapper:

If you've determined that the flapper is the cause of the running toilet, follow these steps to fix it:

a. Turn Off Water Supply:

- Locate the shut-off valve near the base of the toilet and turn it clockwise to shut off the water supply.

b. Flush and Empty Tank:

- Flush the toilet to drain the tank and remove any remaining water using a sponge or towel.

c. Inspect Flapper:

- Check the flapper for signs of wear, damage, or debris that may be preventing it from sealing properly.
- If the flapper is worn or damaged, replace it with a new one that matches the size and type of your flush valve.

d. Adjust Chain:

- Ensure the chain connecting the flush lever to the flapper is the proper length and not kinked or tangled.
- Adjust the chain so that it has a slight slack when the flush lever is at rest, allowing the flapper to seal completely.

e. Test and Observe:

- Turn the water supply back on and flush the toilet, observing the flapper's movement and seal.
- If the flapper seals properly and the running stops, the issue has been resolved.

3. Adjusting the Fill Valve:

If the fill valve is causing the running toilet, you may need to adjust the water level or replace the valve entirely.

a. Adjust Water Level:

- Locate the adjustment screw or clip on the fill valve, which is usually near the top of the valve.
- Turn the adjustment screw clockwise to lower the water level or counterclockwise to raise it.
- Adjust the water level so that it is about 1/2 inch below the top of the overflow tube.

b. Replace Fill Valve:
- If adjusting the water level doesn't solve the problem, the fill valve may need to be replaced.
- Turn off the water supply and flush the toilet to empty the tank.
- Disconnect the supply line and remove the old fill valve by unscrewing the lock nut at the base.
- Install the new fill valve according to the manufacturer's instructions, making sure to adjust the water level properly.

4. Checking the Overflow Tube:

If the water level in the tank is too high, causing water to flow into the overflow tube, you'll need to adjust the fill valve as described above. Additionally:

a. Check for Obstructions:
- Ensure that the overflow tube is not clogged with debris, which can cause water to back up and continually flow into the bowl.

b. Inspect Fill Tube:
- Check that the small flexible fill tube connected to the fill valve is directed into the overflow tube and not spraying water elsewhere in the tank.

5. Testing and Monitoring:

After making any repairs or adjustments, it's important to test the toilet and monitor its performance.

a. Flush and Observe:
- Flush the toilet and observe the flushing mechanism to ensure all components are working properly and the running has stopped.

b. Monitor for Leaks:
- Check for any signs of leaks around the base of the toilet or near the tank connections.

- If leaks are present, tighten connections or replace any damaged components as necessary.

c. Periodic Maintenance:

- To prevent future running toilet issues, perform regular maintenance on your toilet.
- This includes cleaning the tank components, replacing worn parts, and periodically checking for leaks or other issues.

By following these steps and identifying the specific cause of your running toilet, you can often resolve the issue without the need for professional assistance. However, if the problem persists or you encounter any difficulties during the repair process, don't hesitate to contact a licensed plumber for further guidance or to handle the repair safely and effectively.

Fixing a running toilet promptly not only saves water and reduces your utility bills but also prevents potential water damage and ensures the proper functioning of your plumbing system.

Replacing a Water Heater

A water heater is an essential appliance in any home, providing hot water for various daily tasks such as bathing, cooking, and cleaning. Over time, water heaters can become less efficient, develop leaks, or stop working altogether. When this happens, replacing the water heater is often the most cost-effective solution. In this section, we'll walk you through the process of replacing a water heater.

1. Choosing a New Water Heater:
   Before replacing your water heater, you'll need to select a new unit that meets your household's needs.
   a. Fuel Type:
   • Consider the fuel type of your current water heater (electric, gas, or propane) and decide if you want to stick with the same type or switch to a different one.
   • If switching fuel types, ensure that the necessary infrastructure and connections are available in your home.
   b. Tank vs. Tankless:
   • Decide between a traditional tank-style water heater or a tankless (on-demand) model.
   • Tank-style heaters store and continuously heat a large volume of water, while tankless heaters heat water instantly as needed.
   c. Size and Capacity:
   • Determine the appropriate size and capacity of your new water heater based on your household's hot water needs.
   • Consider factors such as the number of people in your home, the number of bathrooms, and your typical hot water usage patterns.

2. Preparing for Replacement:

Before beginning the replacement process, take the necessary safety precautions and gather the required tools and materials.

a. Turn Off Utilities:

- For an electric water heater, turn off the power at the circuit breaker.
- For a gas water heater, turn off the gas supply valve and disconnect the gas line.

b. Drain the Old Water Heater:

- Turn off the cold water supply valve to the water heater.
- Attach a garden hose to the drain valve at the bottom of the tank and direct the other end to a floor drain or outside.
- Open the drain valve and allow the tank to empty completely.

c. Disconnect the Old Water Heater:

- Disconnect the cold and hot water supply lines from the top of the water heater.
- For a gas water heater, disconnect the vent pipe from the top of the unit.

d. Remove the Old Water Heater:

- Carefully remove the old water heater from its location, taking care not to damage any surrounding pipes or structures.
- If the old unit is heavy or difficult to maneuver, enlist the help of an assistant.

3. Installing the New Water Heater:

With the old unit removed, you can now install the new water heater.

a. Position the New Water Heater:

- Place the new water heater in the same location as the old one, ensuring it is level and stable.
- If necessary, adjust the water heater's feet or use shims to level the unit.

b. Connect the Water Lines:
- Attach the cold and hot water supply lines to the corresponding connections on the top of the new water heater.
- Use Teflon tape or pipe joint compound on the threads to ensure a tight, leak-free seal.

c. Connect the Pressure Relief Valve:
- Install the pressure relief valve (if not already installed) on the designated opening near the top of the water heater.
- Attach a discharge pipe to the pressure relief valve and direct it downward to within 6 inches of the floor.

d. Connect the Fuel Source:
- For an electric water heater, connect the electrical wires according to the manufacturer's wiring diagram.
- For a gas water heater, reconnect the gas line and vent pipe, following the manufacturer's instructions and local building codes.

4. Testing and Finishing Up:

After installing the new water heater, it's crucial to test the unit for proper function and check for any leaks.

a. Fill the Tank:
- Turn on the cold water supply valve and allow the tank to fill completely.
- Open a hot water faucet in your home to release any trapped air in the lines.

b. Turn On the Fuel Source:
- For an electric water heater, turn on the circuit breaker.
- For a gas water heater, turn on the gas supply valve and relight the pilot light (if applicable) according to the manufacturer's instructions.

c. Check for Leaks:
- Inspect all the connections and joints for any signs of leaks.
- If leaks are detected, turn off the fuel source and water supply, and tighten the connections or replace any faulty components.

d. Adjust Temperature:
- Set the water heater's temperature to your desired level (usually around 120°F) using the thermostat control.
- Allow the water heater to heat up fully and test the hot water at various faucets throughout your home.

5. Disposal and Maintenance:

After successfully installing and testing the new water heater, properly dispose of the old unit and establish a maintenance routine.

a. Dispose of the Old Water Heater:
- Check with your local authorities for the proper disposal method for your old water heater.
- Many communities have specific guidelines or programs for recycling large appliances.

b. Insulate Pipes:
- To improve energy efficiency and prevent heat loss, insulate the hot water pipes leading from the water heater to your home's fixtures.

c. Schedule Regular Maintenance:
- Establish a regular maintenance schedule to ensure your new water heater continues to function efficiently and safely.
- This may include annual flushing, anode rod replacement, and checking the pressure relief valve.

By following these steps and adhering to the manufacturer's instructions and local building codes, you can successfully replace your water heater and enjoy a reliable supply of hot water for your household. If at any point you feel uncertain about the process or encounter complications, don't hesitate to contact a licensed plumber for professional assistance.

Remember to prioritize safety, take your time, and double-check your work to ensure a proper and leak-free installation. With a new, efficient water heater in place, you can look forward to lower energy bills and a dependable hot water supply for years to come.

Soldering Copper Pipes

Soldering is a essential skill for anyone working with copper plumbing. It involves joining copper pipes and fittings using a torch, solder, and flux to create a strong, leak-free connection. Soldering is commonly used in water supply lines, heating systems, and refrigeration units. In this section, we'll guide you through the process of soldering copper pipes, including the tools and materials needed, preparation steps, and the soldering technique itself.

1. Safety Precautions:

Before beginning any soldering project, it's crucial to prioritize safety to prevent injuries and property damage.

a. Protect Yourself:

- Wear protective gloves, safety glasses, and a long-sleeved shirt to protect your hands, eyes, and skin from heat and debris.
- Ensure proper ventilation in your work area to avoid inhaling fumes from the soldering process.

b. Manage Fire Risk:

- Keep a fire extinguisher nearby in case of any accidental ignition of surrounding materials.
- Remove any flammable materials from your work area, such as paper, fabric, or chemicals.

c. Avoid Water Damage:

- Turn off the water supply to the pipes you'll be soldering and drain any remaining water from the lines.
- Place a heat-resistant cloth or board behind the pipes to protect walls or other surfaces from heat damage.

2. Tools and Materials:

To solder copper pipes successfully, you'll need the following tools and materials:

a. Torch:

- Use a propane or MAPP gas torch designed for soldering.
- Ensure you have enough fuel and that the torch is in good working condition.

b. Solder:

- Choose a lead-free solder that is appropriate for your application (e.g., water supply lines).
- Common solder types include 95/5 (tin-antimony) and 97/3 (tin-copper).

c. Flux:

- Use a water-soluble flux paste or liquid to help the solder flow and adhere to the copper.
- Avoid using acid-based fluxes, as they can corrode the copper over time.

d. Other Tools:

- Have a tubing cutter, emery cloth (or wire brush), flux brush, and a clean rag on hand.
- Keep a bucket of water nearby to cool the joints after soldering.

3. Preparation:

Proper preparation is key to achieving a strong, leak-free solder joint.

a. Cut and Ream Pipes:

- Use a tubing cutter to cut the copper pipes to the desired length.
- Ream the inside edges of the cut pipes with the reaming attachment on the tubing cutter to remove any burrs.

b. Clean and Fit:

- Clean the outside of the pipe ends and the inside of the fittings with emery cloth or a wire brush until they are shiny.

- Ensure the pipes fit snugly into the fittings, leaving no gaps.

c. Apply Flux:

- Use a flux brush to apply a thin, even layer of flux to the cleaned pipe ends and the inside of the fittings.
- The flux will help the solder flow and create a stronger bond.

4. Soldering Technique:

With the preparation complete, you can now begin the soldering process.

a. Heat the Joint:

- Ignite your torch and adjust the flame so that the blue cone at the tip is about 1/2 inch long.
- Apply the flame to the fitting, focusing on the bottom and moving the flame around the joint to heat it evenly.
- Avoid overheating the joint, as this can cause the flux to burn off and the solder to flow poorly.

b. Apply Solder:

- Touch the end of the solder to the joint at the point where the pipe meets the fitting.
- As the joint reaches the correct temperature, the solder will melt and be drawn into the joint by capillary action.
- Continue applying solder around the entire circumference of the joint until a small bead of solder appears around the edge.

c. Cool and Wipe:

- Remove the flame and allow the joint to cool naturally for a few seconds.
- Wipe the joint with a clean rag to remove any excess flux or solder.
- Avoid disturbing the joint until it has cooled completely.

5. Inspection and Testing:

After soldering, it's essential to inspect your work and test the joints for leaks.

a. Visual Inspection:

- Examine each soldered joint for a complete, even solder ring around the entire circumference.
- Look for any gaps, pinholes, or lumpy solder, which may indicate an improper joint.

b. Pressure Test:

- Turn on the water supply and check for any leaks at the soldered joints.
- If leaks are detected, you may need to re-solder the joint or replace the fitting.

c. Clean Up:

- Once you've confirmed that all joints are leak-free, clean the pipes and fittings with a damp rag to remove any remaining flux or debris.
- Dispose of any scrap materials, such as cut pipe pieces or used solder, properly.

By following these steps and practicing proper safety precautions, you can successfully solder copper pipes and create strong, leak-free connections. Remember to take your time, maintain a steady hand, and keep the torch moving to avoid overheating the joints.

If you're new to soldering, it's a good idea to practice on scrap pieces of copper pipe before tackling a real plumbing project. With experience, you'll develop a feel for the correct soldering temperature and technique, making the process easier and more efficient.

If at any point you feel unsure about your abilities or encounter a particularly challenging soldering project, don't hesitate to consult a professional plumber for guidance or assistance. Proper soldering is essential for maintaining a safe, reliable, and leak-free plumbing system in your home.

Chapter 4
Carpentry and Woodworking
Building Simple Shelves and Bookcases

Creating custom shelves and bookcases is a rewarding woodworking project that can add both functional storage and aesthetic appeal to your home. Whether you're looking to organize your book collection, display decorative items, or create additional storage space, building simple shelves and bookcases is a great way to put your carpentry skills to use. In this section, we'll walk you through the process of designing, planning, and constructing basic shelves and bookcases.

1. Planning and Design:
   Before starting any woodworking project, it's crucial to plan and design your shelves or bookcase to ensure a successful outcome.
   a. Determine Size and Location:
   • Measure the space where you intend to place the shelves or bookcase, noting the width, height, and depth of the available area.
   • Consider the size of the items you plan to store on the shelves, such as books, picture frames, or decorative objects.
   b. Sketch Your Design:
   • Create a rough sketch of your shelves or bookcase, including the number of shelves, spacing between shelves, and overall dimensions.
   • Decide on the style and aesthetic you want to achieve, such as a simple utilitarian design or a more decorative approach.
   c. Choose Materials:
   • Select the appropriate wood species for your project, considering factors such as durability, appearance, and cost.
   • Common wood choices for shelves and bookcases include pine, oak, maple, and MDF (medium-density fiberboard).

2. Tools and Materials:

To build simple shelves and bookcases, you'll need the following tools and materials:

a. Tools:
- Measuring tape, pencil, and carpenter's square
- Circular saw or table saw for cutting wood to size
- Drill and drill bits for creating pilot holes and driving screws
- Level for ensuring shelves are straight and even
- Sander (optional) for smoothing rough edges and surfaces

b. Materials:
- Wood boards for shelves and vertical supports (thickness and width depending on your design)
- Wood screws or nails for assembling the components
- Wood glue for added strength and stability
- Sandpaper (various grits) for smoothing surfaces
- Wood stain, paint, or varnish (optional) for finishing the shelves or bookcase

3. Cutting and Preparation:

With your design and materials in hand, it's time to start cutting and preparing the individual components of your shelves or bookcase.

a. Cut Shelves and Supports:
- Using your measurements and design sketch, cut the wood boards to the appropriate lengths for the shelves and vertical supports.
- Ensure all cuts are straight and precise to maintain a professional appearance and proper fit.

b. Sand and Smooth:
- Use sandpaper to smooth any rough edges or surfaces on the cut pieces, progressing from coarser to finer grits for a smooth finish.
- Pay extra attention to the visible edges and surfaces that will be most noticeable once the shelves or bookcase is assembled.

c. Pre-drill Pilot Holes:
- To prevent splitting and ensure accurate assembly, pre-drill pilot holes for screws at the locations where the shelves will attach to the vertical supports.
- Use a drill bit slightly smaller than the diameter of the screws you'll be using.

4. Assembly:

With all the components cut and prepared, it's time to assemble your shelves or bookcase.

a. Attach Vertical Supports:
- Begin by attaching the vertical supports to the top and bottom shelves, ensuring they are perpendicular and aligned properly.
- Use wood glue and screws (or nails) to secure the supports, driving the fasteners through the pre-drilled pilot holes.

b. Install Shelves:
- Place the remaining shelves onto the vertical supports, checking for level and even spacing.
- Secure each shelf to the supports using wood glue and screws (or nails), driving the fasteners through the pre-drilled pilot holes.

c. Reinforce and Square:
- As you assemble the shelves or bookcase, periodically check for square by measuring the diagonals and adjusting as needed.
- Consider adding a back panel to your bookcase for added stability and rigidity, especially if it will be holding heavy items.

5. Finishing Touches:

Once your shelves or bookcase is assembled, it's time to add any finishing touches to enhance its appearance and protect the wood.

a. Fill and Sand:

- If necessary, fill any visible screw holes or imperfections with wood filler, allowing it to dry completely.
- Sand the filled areas smooth, blending them with the surrounding surface.

b. Stain, Paint, or Varnish:

- Depending on your desired aesthetic, you may choose to stain, paint, or varnish your shelves or bookcase.
- Follow the manufacturer's instructions for application and drying times, ensuring proper ventilation in your work area.

c. Add Decorative Elements:

- Consider adding decorative elements such as molding, trim, or hardware to enhance the appearance of your shelves or bookcase.
- Be creative and personalize your project to suit your individual style and preferences.

6. Installation and Use:

With your shelves or bookcase complete, it's time to install it in its designated location and put it to use.

a. Secure to Wall (Optional):

- If desired, secure the shelves or bookcase to the wall for added stability, especially if it will be holding heavy items or if you have young children in your home.
- Use appropriate wall anchors and fasteners, following the manufacturer's instructions for your specific wall type.

b. Arrange Items:

- Carefully arrange your books, decorative items, or storage containers on the shelves, taking care not to overload them.
- Consider grouping items by size, color, or theme for a cohesive and organized appearance.

c. Maintain and Clean:
- Regularly dust and clean your shelves or bookcase to keep it looking its best and to protect the wood from damage.
- Periodically check for any loose screws or connections, tightening them as needed to maintain structural integrity.

By following these steps and using your creativity and attention to detail, you can successfully build simple shelves and bookcases that add both function and style to your living spaces. Remember to prioritize safety, take your time, and measure carefully to ensure a high-quality finished product.

As you gain experience and confidence in your carpentry skills, you can explore more advanced shelving and bookcase designs, incorporating features such as adjustable shelves, glass doors, or integrated lighting. The possibilities are endless, and the satisfaction of creating custom storage solutions for your home is truly rewarding.

Installing Crown Molding and Baseboards

Crown molding and baseboards are decorative trim elements that can add a touch of elegance and refinement to any room. Crown molding is installed at the junction between walls and ceilings, while baseboards are installed at the base of walls, where they meet the floor. Both serve to conceal gaps, create a finished appearance, and provide a decorative transition between surfaces. In this section, we'll guide you through the process of installing crown molding and baseboards.

1. Planning and Preparation:

Before beginning your installation, it's essential to plan your project and prepare your work area.

a. Measure and Calculate:

- Measure the length of each wall where you'll be installing the molding or baseboard, adding a few extra inches to account for cuts and waste.
- Calculate the total linear footage needed and purchase enough material to complete your project.

b. Choose Materials:

- Select the appropriate style and material for your crown molding and baseboards, considering factors such as the room's décor, budget, and installation difficulty.
- Common materials include wood, MDF (medium-density fiberboard), and polyurethane.

c. Gather Tools and Supplies:

- Assemble the necessary tools, including a miter saw, coping saw, nail gun (or hammer and finish nails), measuring tape, pencil, and safety glasses.
- Have wood glue, caulk, sandpaper, and paint or stain on hand for finishing touches.

2. Cutting and Fitting:

Accurate cuts and a proper fit are crucial for a professional-looking installation.

a. Miter Cuts for Corners:

- Use a miter saw to cut 45-degree angles on the ends of the molding or baseboard pieces that will meet at inside and outside corners.
- For inside corners, cut one piece square and the other at a 45-degree angle to create a cope joint.

b. Coping Inside Corners (Crown Molding):

- To achieve a seamless fit at inside corners, use a coping saw to cut along the profile of the molding, following the 45-degree miter cut.
- This technique allows the molding pieces to nest together, creating a tight, professional-looking joint.

c. Dry Fit and Adjust:

- Before attaching the molding or baseboards, dry fit each piece to ensure a proper fit and make any necessary adjustments.
- Trim pieces as needed for a snug fit, using a miter saw or coping saw for precise cuts.

3. Installation:

With your pieces cut and fitted, it's time to install the crown molding and baseboards.

a. Locate Studs and Mark Position:

- Use a stud finder to locate and mark the position of wall studs, which will provide a secure anchoring point for the molding and baseboards.
- For crown molding, also mark the bottom edge position on the wall as a guide for installation.

b. Attach Molding and Baseboards:

- Begin at one end of the room and work your way around, attaching each piece securely to the wall studs.

- Use a nail gun or hammer and finish nails to fasten the molding and baseboards in place, ensuring they are straight and level.
- For crown molding, use a helper or support blocks to hold the pieces in place while nailing.

c. Cope Inside Corners (Baseboards):

- For baseboard inside corners, use a coping saw to cut along the profile of the baseboard, similar to the technique used for crown molding.
- This will create a seamless, professional-looking joint where the baseboard pieces meet.

4. Finishing Touches:

After installation, add finishing touches to enhance the appearance and durability of your crown molding and baseboards.

a. Fill Nail Holes and Gaps:

- Use wood filler to fill any visible nail holes or minor gaps, allowing it to dry completely.
- Sand the filled areas smooth, blending them with the surrounding surface.

b. Caulk Seams and Joints:

- Apply a thin bead of caulk along the top and bottom edges of the molding and baseboards, as well as at any joints or seams.
- Use a damp finger or caulk smoothing tool to smooth the caulk for a clean, finished appearance.

c. Paint or Stain:

- Once the filler and caulk have dried, paint or stain the molding and baseboards to match your desired color scheme.
- Apply the finish according to the manufacturer's instructions, using painter's tape to protect adjacent surfaces if necessary.

5. Maintenance and Care:

To keep your newly installed crown molding and baseboards looking their best, follow these maintenance and care tips:

a. Regular Cleaning:

- Dust and clean the molding and baseboards regularly to prevent the buildup of dirt and grime.
- Use a soft, damp cloth or a vacuum with a soft brush attachment to remove dust and cobwebs.

b. Touch-ups and Repairs:

- Periodically inspect the molding and baseboards for any signs of damage, such as cracks, chips, or loose sections.
- Make repairs as needed, using wood filler, caulk, or touch-up paint to maintain a seamless appearance.

c. Avoid Moisture Damage:

- In areas prone to moisture, such as bathrooms or kitchens, consider using moisture-resistant materials or applying a protective finish to prevent water damage.
- Wipe up any spills or splashes promptly to avoid staining or warping the molding and baseboards.

By following these steps and paying attention to the details, you can successfully install crown molding and baseboards that enhance the beauty and value of your home. Remember to measure carefully, cut precisely, and take your time to ensure a professional-looking result.

As you gain experience and confidence in your carpentry skills, you can explore more intricate molding profiles and techniques, such as layering multiple moldings or creating custom designs. The possibilities are endless, and the satisfaction of adding a touch of elegance to your living spaces is truly rewarding.

Hanging Interior Doors

Interior doors serve both functional and aesthetic purposes in a home, providing privacy, noise reduction, and a finished appearance to doorways. Hanging a new interior door or replacing an existing one is a common carpentry project that requires attention to detail and precise measurements. In this section, we'll walk you through the process of hanging an interior door, including preparing the opening, installing the door frame, and attaching the door itself.

1. Measuring and Selecting the Door:

Before beginning the installation process, it's crucial to accurately measure the door opening and select the appropriate door size and style.

a. Measure the Opening:

- Use a tape measure to determine the width, height, and thickness of the door opening.
- Measure the width at the top, middle, and bottom of the opening, and use the smallest measurement to ensure a proper fit.
- Measure the height from the floor to the top of the opening at both sides, and use the larger measurement.

b. Choose the Door:

- Based on your measurements, select a door that is slightly smaller than the opening to allow for shimming and adjustments.
- Consider factors such as the door's material, style, and any additional features like glass inserts or pre-drilled hinge holes.

c. Gather Tools and Materials:

- Assemble the necessary tools, including a level, hammer, chisel, screwdriver, drill, saw, and shims.
- Have the door, door frame (if not pre-hung), hinges, screws, and any additional hardware on hand.

2. Preparing the Opening:

Before installing the door frame, ensure the opening is properly prepared and free from any obstructions.

a. Remove Old Door and Frame:

- If replacing an existing door, carefully remove the old door and frame, taking note of any shims or spacers used for proper alignment.
- Remove any nails, screws, or debris from the opening, and fill any holes or cracks with wood filler.

b. Check for Plumb and Level:

- Use a level to check that the opening is plumb (vertically straight) and level (horizontally straight).
- If necessary, make adjustments to the opening by shimming or trimming the framing to ensure a square and plumb opening.

c. Install Subfloor and Jamb Liner (if needed):

- If the opening doesn't have a subfloor or if the existing subfloor is damaged, install a new subfloor to provide a stable base for the door frame.
- If using a pre-hung door with a jamb liner, install the liner according to the manufacturer's instructions.

3. Installing the Door Frame:

With the opening prepared, it's time to install the door frame, which consists of the jamb, head, and threshold.

a. Assemble the Frame:

- If using a pre-hung door, the frame will already be assembled. If not, assemble the frame according to the manufacturer's instructions.
- Ensure that the frame is square and that the jamb legs are the appropriate length for the opening.

b. Position and Shim the Frame:

- Place the frame into the opening, ensuring it is plumb, level, and square.

79

- Use shims to adjust the frame's position, inserting them behind the hinges and at various points along the jamb to maintain proper alignment.

c. Secure the Frame:

- Once the frame is properly positioned, secure it to the opening using finish nails or screws.
- Drive the fasteners through the frame and into the rough opening, using shims to maintain the frame's position as needed.

4. Hanging the Door:

With the frame installed, you can now hang the door itself.

a. Attach Hinges to Door:

- If the hinges aren't already attached to the door, position them according to the manufacturer's specifications and pre-drill pilot holes.
- Secure the hinges to the door using screws, ensuring they are snug but not over-tightened.

b. Mount Door in Frame:

- Carefully lift the door and position it in the frame, aligning the hinges with the mortises in the frame.
- Insert the hinge pins to secure the door in place, using a hammer to gently tap them in if necessary.

c. Adjust and Secure:

- Check that the door opens and closes smoothly, and that it fits properly within the frame.
- Make any necessary adjustments by shimming or planing the door or frame until the fit is satisfactory.
- Once the door is properly aligned, secure the hinges to the frame using screws.

5. Installing Hardware and Finishing:

With the door hung, you can now install the hardware and add any finishing touches.

a. Install Lockset and Handles:

- Follow the manufacturer's instructions to install the lockset and door handles, ensuring they are properly aligned and securely fastened.
- Test the operation of the lock and handles to ensure smooth functionality.

b. Attach Door Stop and Weather Stripping:

- Install a door stop on the frame to prevent the door from swinging too far and damaging the wall.
- If desired, add weather stripping around the perimeter of the door to reduce drafts and improve energy efficiency.

c. Paint or Stain:

- If the door and frame are unfinished, apply paint or stain according to your preference and the room's décor.
- Be sure to follow the manufacturer's instructions for application and drying times.

6. Maintenance and Troubleshooting:

To keep your newly hung door functioning properly, perform regular maintenance and troubleshoot any issues that may arise.

a. Lubricate Moving Parts:

- Periodically lubricate the hinges, lock, and handles with a silicone-based lubricant to ensure smooth operation and prevent squeaking.

b. Tighten Loose Hardware:

- Check for any loose screws or hardware, and tighten them as needed to maintain the door's stability and functionality.

c. Adjust Alignment:

- If the door begins to stick, rub, or not close properly, adjust the alignment by shimming or planing the door or frame as needed.

- In some cases, you may need to remove the door and reposition the hinges or adjust the frame to correct alignment issues.

By following these steps and paying close attention to measurements and alignment, you can successfully hang an interior door that functions smoothly and enhances the look of your home. Remember to take your time, use the proper tools, and don't hesitate to make adjustments as needed to achieve the best possible fit.

As you gain experience and confidence in your carpentry skills, you can tackle more complex door installations, such as pocket doors, French doors, or doors with intricate moldings and hardware. With practice and attention to detail, hanging interior doors can become a rewarding and satisfying DIY project.

Repairing Squeaky Floors

Squeaky floors can be a common and annoying problem in many homes. The squeaks and creaks often occur when floorboards rub against each other or against the subfloor, usually due to loose nails, changes in humidity, or general wear and tear. Fortunately, there are several methods you can use to repair squeaky floors, depending on the type of flooring and the accessibility of the problem area. In this section, we'll explore various techniques for identifying and fixing squeaky floors.

1. Identifying the Squeak:

The first step in repairing a squeaky floor is to pinpoint the exact location of the squeak.

a. Walk the Floor:

- Walk slowly across the affected area, listening carefully for the squeak and feeling for any movement underfoot.
- Have a helper stand in the room below (if applicable) to help identify the location of the squeak from underneath.

b. Mark the Spot:

- Once you've located the squeak, place a piece of tape or a sticky note on the floor to mark the spot for easy reference.
- If you have access to the subfloor from below, mark the corresponding spot on the ceiling or joists.

2. Fixing Squeaks from Above:

If you can't access the subfloor from below, or if you have a finished ceiling underneath, you can try fixing the squeak from above.

a. Talcum Powder or Graphite:

- For minor squeaks caused by floorboards rubbing together, try sprinkling talcum powder or graphite lubricant between the boards.

- Work the powder into the cracks using a fine-bristled brush, then wipe away any excess.

b. Nail or Screw Down Loose Boards:

- If the squeak is caused by a loose floorboard, try driving a finishing nail or trim screw through the board and into the subfloor or joist.
- Countersink the nail or screw slightly below the surface of the board to prevent snagging.
- Fill the hole with wood putty and sand it smooth once dry.

c. Squeak-Fixing Kits:

- For more stubborn squeaks, consider using a squeak-fixing kit, which typically includes a joist-finding bit, a pilot bit, and specially designed screws.
- Follow the manufacturer's instructions to locate the joist, drill a pilot hole, and drive the screw through the floorboard and into the joist.

3. Fixing Squeaks from Below:

If you have access to the subfloor from below, such as in a basement or crawl space, you can often fix squeaks more easily.

a. Shims:

- If the squeak is caused by a gap between the subfloor and the joist, cut a shim to fit snugly into the gap.
- Apply wood glue to the shim and tap it into place using a hammer, being careful not to drive it in too far.
- Once the glue has dried, trim any excess shim material flush with the joist using a utility knife.

b. Construction Adhesive:

- For squeaks caused by a loose subfloor, apply a bead of construction adhesive along the joist where it meets the subfloor.
- Press the subfloor firmly down onto the adhesive and hold it in place with temporary bracing or weights until the adhesive has dried.

c. Screws or Nails:
- If the subfloor is still loose after applying adhesive, secure it to the joist using screws or nails.
- Drive the fasteners through the subfloor and into the joist at regular intervals, being careful not to puncture any wiring or plumbing.

4. Fixing Squeaks in Carpeted Floors:

Repairing squeaks in carpeted floors can be a bit more challenging, but it's still possible without removing the carpet.

a. Locate the Joist:
- Use a stud finder or tap on the floor to locate the nearest joist to the squeak.
- Mark the location of the joist with a piece of tape or a chalk line.

b. Drive Screws or Nails:
- Using a power drill or hammer, drive a screw or nail through the carpet and padding and into the subfloor and joist.
- Be sure to use a screw or nail that is long enough to penetrate the joist, but not so long that it punctures the floor above.

c. Conceal the Repair:
- After driving the screw or nail, use a pair of pliers to grasp the carpet fibers around the head of the fastener and pull them over the head to conceal it.
- If necessary, use a carpet repair kit to patch any visible holes or damage to the carpet.

5. Preventing Future Squeaks:

To minimize the occurrence of squeaky floors in the future, consider the following preventative measures:

a. Maintain Consistent Humidity:
- Changes in humidity can cause wood flooring to expand and contract, leading to squeaks and creaks.

- Use a humidifier or dehumidifier to maintain a consistent humidity level in your home, ideally between 30-50%.

b. Secure Loose Flooring:

- Regularly inspect your floors for any signs of loose boards or subfloor, and secure them promptly using the methods described above.

c. Use Proper Fasteners:

- When installing new flooring or making repairs, be sure to use the appropriate size and type of fasteners, such as screws or ring-shank nails, to minimize the risk of loosening over time.

By following these techniques and taking a systematic approach to identifying and repairing squeaky floors, you can restore peace and quiet to your home. Remember to work carefully and methodically, and don't hesitate to consult a professional carpenter or flooring specialist if you encounter a particularly stubborn squeak or are unsure about any aspect of the repair process.

With a little patience and effort, you can enjoy squeak-free floors that will stand the test of time and contribute to a more comfortable and inviting living space.

Creating a Custom Cutting Board

A custom cutting board is a practical and attractive addition to any kitchen, providing a durable surface for food preparation while also serving as a stylish décor piece. Making your own cutting board allows you to choose the perfect size, shape, and wood type to suit your needs and preferences. In this section, we'll guide you through the process of creating a custom cutting board, from selecting the wood to finishing and maintaining your board.

1. Choosing the Wood:
   The first step in creating a custom cutting board is selecting the appropriate wood type.
   a. Hardwoods:
   - Choose a hardwood species that is dense, durable, and resistant to scratches and moisture.
   - Popular options include maple, cherry, walnut, oak, and teak.
   - Avoid softwoods like pine or cedar, which are more prone to damage and may impart unwanted flavors to food.
   b. Grain Pattern:
   - Consider the grain pattern of the wood when making your selection.
   - Close-grained woods like maple and cherry are less likely to trap food particles and bacteria.
   - More porous woods like oak may require more frequent cleaning and maintenance.
   c. Aesthetics:
   - Think about the overall look you want to achieve with your cutting board.
   - Different wood species offer a range of colors and grain patterns, from the light, uniform appearance of maple to the rich, varied tones of walnut.

2. Preparing the Wood:

Once you've chosen your wood, it's time to prepare it for the cutting board.

a. Cutting to Size:

- Determine the desired dimensions of your cutting board and cut the wood to size using a table saw or circular saw.
- For a standard cutting board, a thickness of 1 to 1.5 inches is generally suitable.

b. Planing and Sanding:

- Use a planer or jointer to ensure that the wood is flat and even on all sides.
- Sand the wood progressively with increasing grit sandpaper (e.g., 60, 120, 220) to achieve a smooth, polished surface.

c. Laminating (optional):

- For a thicker or larger cutting board, you may need to laminate multiple pieces of wood together.
- Apply a food-safe wood glue between the pieces and clamp them tightly together, allowing the glue to dry completely before proceeding.

3. Designing the Cutting Board:

With the wood prepared, you can now focus on the design elements of your custom cutting board.

a. Shape:

- Decide on the shape of your cutting board, such as rectangular, square, round, or a unique custom shape.
- Use a template or freehand design to trace the desired shape onto the wood.

b. Handles or Cutouts:

- Consider adding handles or finger grooves to your cutting board for easier handling and transport.
- You can also incorporate decorative cutouts or inlays to personalize your board.

c. Routing and Sanding:

- Use a router to shape the edges of your cutting board and create any desired handles or cutouts.
- Sand the routed areas smooth, paying extra attention to any curves or detailed elements.

4. Finishing the Cutting Board:

To protect your cutting board and enhance its appearance, you'll need to apply a food-safe finish.

a. Oil Finish:

- Apply a food-grade mineral oil or a specially formulated cutting board oil to the surface of the board.
- Allow the oil to soak into the wood for several hours or overnight, then wipe away any excess with a clean cloth.
- Re-oil the board periodically to maintain its moisture resistance and prevent cracking or warping.

b. Wax Finish (optional):

- For added protection and sheen, you can apply a layer of beeswax or a food-safe wood wax over the oil finish.
- Melt the wax and apply it to the board using a clean cloth, buffing it into the surface in a circular motion.

c. Personalization:

- If desired, you can personalize your cutting board by engraving or branding a name, monogram, or design into the wood.
- Use a wood-burning tool or a custom branding iron to create your personalized mark.

5. Maintaining Your Cutting Board:

To keep your custom cutting board in top condition, follow these maintenance tips:

a. Cleaning:

- After each use, wash your cutting board with warm, soapy water and scrub gently with a soft brush or sponge.

- Rinse the board thoroughly and dry it immediately with a clean towel to prevent moisture damage.

b. Oiling:

- Every few weeks or whenever the board starts to look dry, apply a fresh coat of food-grade mineral oil or cutting board oil.
- Allow the oil to soak in for several hours, then wipe away any excess.

c. Storage:

- Store your cutting board in a dry, well-ventilated area away from direct sunlight or heat sources.
- Avoid storing the board in a damp or humid environment, which can lead to warping or mold growth.

d. Repairs:

- If your cutting board develops any cracks, splits, or deep gouges, sand the affected area smooth and re-oil the board to prevent further damage.
- For more serious damage, you may need to glue and clamp the board or have it professionally repaired.

Creating a custom cutting board is a rewarding woodworking project that combines practicality with creativity. By selecting high-quality hardwoods, designing a functional and attractive shape, and finishing the board with food-safe oils or waxes, you can craft a unique and long-lasting kitchen accessory that will be a joy to use and display.

Remember to take your time, work carefully, and always prioritize safety when using power tools or sharp blades. With a little patience and attention to detail, you can create a beautiful and functional custom cutting board that will serve you well for years to come.

Chapter 5
Painting and Wallpapering
Preparing Surfaces for Painting

Proper surface preparation is crucial for achieving a smooth, long-lasting, and professional-looking paint job. Whether you're painting walls, ceilings, trim, or furniture, taking the time to thoroughly prepare the surface will ensure better paint adhesion, minimize imperfections, and reduce the need for frequent touch-ups or repainting. In this section, we'll walk you through the essential steps for preparing various surfaces for painting.

1. Cleaning:
   The first step in preparing any surface for painting is to clean it thoroughly.
   a. Walls and Ceilings:
 • Remove dust, cobwebs, and loose debris using a vacuum cleaner with a brush attachment or a microfiber duster.
 • Wash the surface with a solution of mild detergent and warm water to remove any grease, grime, or stains.
 • For stubborn stains, use a specialized cleaning product appropriate for the surface material (e.g., TSP for heavy grease or nicotine stains).
   b. Trim and Woodwork:
 • Clean trim, baseboards, and door/window frames with a degreaser or all-purpose cleaner to remove built-up dirt and oils.
 • For intricate or ornamental woodwork, use a soft-bristled brush to get into crevices and hard-to-reach areas.
   c. Furniture:
 • Remove any hardware, such as knobs or pulls, and clean the piece thoroughly with a degreaser or furniture cleaner.
 • Pay special attention to areas that may have accumulated grease or grime, such as kitchen cabinets or dresser drawers.

2. Repairs:

After cleaning, inspect the surface carefully and make any necessary repairs.

a. Filling Holes and Cracks:

- Use spackling compound or wood filler to fill nail holes, dents, or small cracks in walls, ceilings, or woodwork.
- For larger holes or damage, use a patching compound or joint compound, and apply it with a putty knife or trowel.
- Allow the filler to dry completely, then sand it smooth with fine-grit sandpaper.

b. Fixing Imperfections:

- Address any bubbling, peeling, or cracking paint by scraping away the loose material with a paint scraper or wire brush.
- Sand the edges of the damaged area to create a smooth transition between the old and new paint.
- For severe damage, you may need to remove the paint down to the bare surface and start fresh.

3. Sanding:

Sanding helps to create a smooth, even surface that will allow the new paint to adhere properly.

a. Walls and Ceilings:

- Lightly sand the entire surface with a fine-grit sanding block or sandpaper (120-150 grit) to remove any bumps, ridges, or brush strokes from previous paint jobs.
- For textured surfaces, use a pole sander or a drywall sanding screen to avoid altering the texture.

b. Trim and Woodwork:

- Sand the surface with medium-grit sandpaper (100-120 grit) to remove any remaining finish or roughness.
- Progress to a finer-grit sandpaper (150-180 grit) to achieve a smooth, even surface.

c. Furniture:
- Sand the piece thoroughly with medium-grit sandpaper (120-150 grit) to remove the old finish and create a smooth base for the new paint.
- For intricate details or carvings, use a detail sander or sanding sponge to get into tight spaces.

4. Priming:

Applying a primer before painting helps to seal the surface, improve paint adhesion, and create a uniform base color.

a. Choosing the Right Primer:
- Select a primer appropriate for the surface material and the type of paint you'll be using (e.g., oil-based primer for wood, latex primer for drywall).
- For surfaces with significant stains or color changes, use a stain-blocking primer to prevent bleed-through.

b. Applying the Primer:
- Use a brush, roller, or sprayer to apply the primer evenly across the surface, following the manufacturer's instructions for application and drying times.
- For best results, apply a second coat of primer, especially on porous or heavily stained surfaces.

c. Sanding Between Coats:
- After the primer has dried completely, lightly sand the surface with fine-grit sandpaper (220-240 grit) to remove any brush strokes or imperfections.
- Wipe away any sanding dust with a tack cloth or damp rag before proceeding with paint.

5. Masking and Protecting:

To ensure clean lines and prevent paint from getting on adjacent surfaces, it's important to mask and protect the surrounding areas.

a. Taping:
- Use painter's tape to mask off trim, baseboards, window frames, or any other areas you don't want to paint.
- Press the tape firmly against the surface to create a tight seal and prevent paint from seeping underneath.

b. Covering:
- Cover floors, furniture, and any other nearby surfaces with drop cloths, plastic sheeting, or rosin paper to protect them from paint drips or splatters.
- For outdoor projects, use stakes or weights to secure the coverings and prevent them from blowing away.

c. Ventilation:
- Ensure proper ventilation in the work area by opening windows, using fans, or setting up an exhaust system to remove fumes and dust.
- Wear a respirator or mask when sanding or working with oil-based paints or primers to avoid inhaling harmful particles.

By following these surface preparation steps, you'll create a solid foundation for your painting project and ensure a smoother, more professional-looking finish. Remember to work methodically, allow adequate drying times between steps, and always prioritize safety when working with paints, solvents, or power tools.

As you gain experience and confidence in your painting skills, you can tackle more complex projects, such as faux finishes, murals, or decorative techniques. With proper preparation and attention to detail, you can transform any surface in your home with a fresh, beautiful coat of paint.

Choosing the Right Paint and Tools

Selecting the appropriate paint and tools for your project is essential for achieving a professional-looking, long-lasting finish. The right paint will provide the desired color, sheen, and durability, while the proper tools will ensure efficient and effective application. In this section, we'll guide you through the process of choosing the right paint and tools for your specific needs.

1. Types of Paint:

Understanding the different types of paint available will help you make an informed decision for your project.

a. Latex (Water-Based) Paint:

- Latex paint is the most common type of paint for interior walls and ceilings.
- It offers easy clean-up, low odor, and fast drying times, making it a popular choice for DIY projects.
- Latex paint comes in a variety of finishes, from flat to high-gloss, and is suitable for most surfaces, including drywall, plaster, and wood.

b. Oil-Based Paint:

- Oil-based paint is known for its durability, smooth finish, and excellent coverage.
- It is often used for trim, doors, and cabinetry, as well as for high-moisture areas like bathrooms and kitchens.
- Oil-based paint has a stronger odor and longer drying times compared to latex paint, and it requires mineral spirits or paint thinner for clean-up.

c. Specialty Paints:

- Certain projects may require specialty paints, such as chalk paint for a matte, vintage look or metallic paint for a shimmery, glamorous effect.
- Other specialty paints include high-heat paint for radiators or fireplace surrounds, and anti-mold paint for damp or humid areas.

2. Paint Finishes:

The finish or sheen of your paint will impact the overall look and practicality of your project.

a. Flat or Matte:
- Flat or matte finishes have no shine and are best for hiding surface imperfections.
- They are ideal for low-traffic areas like bedrooms or living rooms, as they are less washable and more prone to showing dirt and scuffs.

b. Eggshell or Satin:
- Eggshell and satin finishes have a slight sheen and offer a balance between durability and aesthetics.
- They are easier to clean than flat finishes and are suitable for moderate-traffic areas like hallways or family rooms.

c. Semi-Gloss or Gloss:
- Semi-gloss and gloss finishes have a high shine and are the most durable and washable options.
- They are best for high-traffic areas, trim, doors, and cabinetry, as they can withstand frequent cleaning and resist moisture.

3. Color Selection:

Choosing the right color is a crucial aspect of any painting project, as it can greatly impact the mood and overall look of a space.

a. Color Schemes:
- Consider the existing colors in the room, such as furniture, flooring, and textiles, and choose a paint color that complements or contrasts with them.
- Use color theory principles to create a harmonious color scheme, such as monochromatic, complementary, or analogous colors.

b. Undertones:
- Pay attention to the undertones of your chosen color, as they can significantly affect how the color appears in different lighting conditions.
- Undertones can be warm (yellow, orange, or red) or cool (green, blue, or purple), and can make a color appear more muted or vibrant.

c. Sampling and Testing:
- Before committing to a color, purchase small samples or swatches and test them on the wall in various lighting conditions throughout the day.
- Apply the samples near trim, flooring, and furniture to see how the color interacts with these elements.

4. Essential Painting Tools:
Having the right tools on hand will make your painting project more efficient and ensure a professional-looking finish.

a. Brushes:
- High-quality brushes with a mix of natural and synthetic bristles are best for latex paint, while natural bristle brushes are best for oil-based paint.
- Choose angled brushes for trim and corners, and flat or straight brushes for large, flat surfaces.

b. Rollers:
- Rollers are essential for covering large areas quickly and evenly.
- Select a roller cover with a nap length appropriate for your surface texture (shorter nap for smooth surfaces, longer nap for rough or textured surfaces).

c. Paint Trays and Liners:
- Paint trays hold the paint and provide a surface for loading your roller.
- Disposable tray liners make clean-up easier and allow for quick color changes.

d. Extension Poles:
- Extension poles attach to your roller or brush and allow you to reach high walls or ceilings without a ladder.
- Look for poles with a sturdy, lightweight construction and a comfortable grip.

e. Cleaning Supplies:
- Have plenty of rags, sponges, and clean water on hand for clean-up.
- For latex paint, soap and water are sufficient, while oil-based paint requires mineral spirits or paint thinner.

5. Additional Tools and Accessories:

Depending on your specific project, you may need additional tools or accessories to achieve the best results.

a. Paint Sprayer:
- A paint sprayer can be a worthwhile investment for large projects or intricate surfaces, as it provides fast, even coverage.
- Choose an airless sprayer for thick paints and large surfaces, or an HVLP (high-volume, low-pressure) sprayer for thinner paints and more detailed work.

b. Painter's Tape:
- High-quality painter's tape is essential for creating clean, sharp lines and preventing paint from seeping onto adjacent surfaces.
- Look for tape with strong adhesion and clean removal properties.

c. Sandpaper and Sanding Tools:
- Various grits of sandpaper and sanding tools, such as sanding blocks or electric sanders, are necessary for preparing surfaces and smoothing between coats.

d. Putty Knife and Spackling Compound:
- A putty knife and spackling compound are used for filling holes, cracks, and imperfections in the surface before painting.

By taking the time to choose the right paint and tools for your project, you'll be well-equipped to achieve a beautiful, professional-looking finish that will stand the test of time. Remember to always read and follow the manufacturer's instructions for application, cleaning, and storage of your painting supplies.

As you gain experience and tackle more complex painting projects, you may find that investing in higher-quality tools and experimenting with different paint types and finishes can help you achieve even better results. With the right knowledge and preparation, you can confidently take on any painting project in your home.

Painting Techniques for a Professional Finish

Achieving a professional-looking paint job requires more than just the right tools and materials; it also involves mastering various painting techniques. By employing these techniques, you can ensure a smooth, even finish, minimize imperfections, and create a polished, long-lasting result. In this section, we'll explore several key painting techniques that will help you achieve a professional finish on your next project.

1. Proper Brush Loading:
   Loading your brush correctly is essential for achieving even coverage and minimizing drips or spatters.
   a. Dipping the Brush:
   - Dip the bristles about 1/3 of the way into the paint, then gently tap the brush against the side of the can to remove excess paint.
   - Avoid wiping the brush against the rim of the can, as this can cause the bristles to become misshapen and lead to uneven application.
   b. Distributing the Paint:
   - After loading the brush, gently brush it back and forth on a piece of scrap wood or cardboard to distribute the paint evenly through the bristles.
   - This will also help to remove any excess paint and ensure a more controlled application.

2. Cutting In:
   Cutting in is the technique used to paint a clean, straight line along the edges of walls, ceilings, and trim without using painter's tape.
   a. Brush Selection:
   - Use a high-quality, angled brush with a fine, tapered edge for cutting in.

- A 2-inch or 2.5-inch brush is typically the most versatile size for cutting in.

b. Loading and Application:

- Load the brush as described above, then tap off the excess paint to prevent drips.
- Start by painting a thin, straight line along the edge, using the angled tip of the brush to guide the paint.
- Work slowly and carefully, reloading the brush as needed and maintaining a wet edge to avoid visible brush strokes.

c. Overlapping:

- After cutting in, overlap the brushed area slightly with your roller to blend the two sections seamlessly.
- This will help to create a smooth, even transition between the cut-in area and the main wall surface.

3. Rolling Techniques:

Using a roller is the most efficient way to cover large areas quickly and evenly.

a. Loading the Roller:

- Pour paint into a tray, filling it about halfway.
- Dip the roller into the paint, then roll it back and forth on the ribbed section of the tray to distribute the paint evenly and remove excess.

b. Applying the Paint:

- Start by painting a large "W" pattern on the wall, about 3 feet wide by 3 feet tall.
- Fill in the spaces between the "W" without lifting the roller, using overlapping strokes to ensure even coverage.
- Continue this process until the entire wall is covered, maintaining a wet edge to avoid visible lap marks.

c. Blending:

- To achieve a smooth, seamless finish, blend each section with the previous one while the paint is still wet.

- Lightly roll over the edges of the previous section, using minimal pressure to avoid creating thick spots or uneven texture.

4. Layering and Multiple Coats:

Applying multiple coats of paint is often necessary to achieve a rich, uniform color and a professional-looking finish.

a. First Coat:
- The first coat of paint, also known as the prime coat, serves as a base for the subsequent coats and helps to cover any imperfections or color variations in the surface.
- Apply the first coat using the rolling technique described above, focusing on even coverage rather than a perfect finish.

b. Second and Third Coats:
- After allowing the first coat to dry completely (refer to the manufacturer's instructions for drying times), apply a second coat using the same techniques.
- If necessary, apply a third coat to achieve the desired depth of color and to ensure a smooth, even finish.

c. Sanding Between Coats (Optional):
- For an ultra-smooth finish, lightly sand the surface with a fine-grit sandpaper (220-grit or higher) between coats.
- This will help to remove any minor imperfections or brush strokes and create a flawless surface for the final coat.

5. Creating Texture:

In some cases, you may want to add texture to your painted surface for visual interest or to conceal imperfections.

a. Stippling:
- Stippling involves using a stipple brush or a textured roller to create a subtle, mottled effect on the painted surface.
- Load the brush or roller with paint, then gently tap or roll it over the surface, using a light, even pressure to create a consistent texture.

b. Rag Rolling:
- Rag rolling is a technique that uses a crumpled or twisted cloth to create a soft, textured pattern on the painted surface.
- Apply a base coat of paint, then lightly dab or roll the cloth over the surface while the paint is still wet, using varying pressure to create depth and dimension.

c. Sponging:
- Sponging involves using a natural or synthetic sponge to create a mottled, textured effect on the painted surface.
- Apply a base coat of paint, then lightly dab the sponge over the surface while the paint is still wet, using a random pattern to create a natural-looking texture.

6. Touch-Ups and Clean-Up:

No matter how carefully you work, minor imperfections or drips may occur. Knowing how to address these issues and properly clean your tools is essential for a professional-looking finish.

a. Touch-Ups:
- After the paint has dried completely, inspect the surface carefully for any missed spots, drips, or imperfections.
- Use a small brush to carefully touch up these areas, blending the new paint seamlessly with the surrounding surface.

b. Cleaning Brushes and Rollers:
- For latex paint, clean your brushes and rollers immediately after use with warm, soapy water.
- For oil-based paint, clean your tools with mineral spirits or paint thinner, then wash them with soap and water.
- Squeeze out excess water and reshape the bristles or fibers before allowing the tools to air dry completely.

c. Disposing of Materials:
- Dispose of any unused paint, primers, or solvents according to your local regulations, as these materials can be hazardous if not handled properly.

- Many communities have designated collection sites or events for disposing of household hazardous waste, including paint and related materials.

By mastering these painting techniques and paying close attention to detail, you can achieve a professional-looking finish on any painting project in your home. Remember to work patiently, maintain a consistent technique, and always prioritize proper preparation and clean-up to ensure the best possible results.

As you gain experience and confidence in your painting skills, don't be afraid to experiment with different techniques, tools, and finishes to create unique and personalized looks for your space. With practice and persistence, you'll be able to tackle increasingly complex painting projects with ease and achieve the polished, professional results you desire.

Removing Old Wallpaper

Removing old wallpaper can be a time-consuming and challenging task, but it's often necessary before painting or applying new wallpaper. Over time, wallpaper can become damaged, outdated, or simply no longer suit your personal style. In this section, we'll guide you through the process of removing old wallpaper, including the tools and techniques needed to make the job as efficient and stress-free as possible.

1. Assessing the Wallpaper:
Before beginning the removal process, it's important to assess the condition and type of wallpaper you're dealing with.
a. Identifying the Type of Wallpaper:
- Determine whether the wallpaper is strippable, peelable, or traditional.
- Strippable wallpaper can be easily removed in large strips without the need for water or chemicals.
- Peelable wallpaper has a top layer that can be peeled off, leaving behind a backing that must be removed separately.
- Traditional wallpaper is the most common and requires water or chemicals to loosen the adhesive before scraping.
b. Evaluating the Condition:
- Check the wallpaper for any signs of damage, such as tears, bubbles, or loose seams.
- If the wallpaper is in poor condition or has been painted over, the removal process may be more challenging and time-consuming.

2. Gathering Tools and Materials:
Having the right tools and materials on hand will make the wallpaper removal process more efficient and effective.
a. Essential Tools:
- Wallpaper scraper or putty knife
- Scoring tool or perforation roller

- Drop cloths or plastic sheeting
- Ladder or step stool
- Bucket and sponge
- Spray bottle

b. Removal Solutions:
- Warm water
- Liquid concentrate wallpaper remover
- Fabric softener (for stubborn adhesive)
- Vinegar (for tough residue)

c. Protective Gear:
- Safety goggles
- Dust mask
- Rubber gloves
- Knee pads (for kneeling on the floor)

3. Preparing the Room:

Before starting the removal process, take steps to protect your floors, furniture, and electrical outlets.

a. Clearing the Space:
- Remove all furniture, decor, and wall hangings from the room.
- If you can't remove larger items, move them to the center of the room and cover them with drop cloths or plastic sheeting.

b. Protecting Floors and Surfaces:
- Cover the floor with drop cloths or plastic sheeting, securing the edges with painter's tape to prevent slipping.
- Remove outlet and switch covers, and cover the openings with painter's tape to prevent water or debris from entering.

c. Ventilating the Area:
- Open windows and use fans to ensure proper ventilation, especially if you'll be using chemical wallpaper removers.

4. Scoring and Wetting the Wallpaper:

To allow the removal solution to penetrate the wallpaper and loosen the adhesive, you'll need to score and wet the surface.

a. Scoring:

- Use a scoring tool or perforation roller to create small holes in the wallpaper surface.
- Work in a circular motion, applying even pressure to ensure the holes are deep enough to allow the removal solution to penetrate.
- Be careful not to press too hard, as this can damage the drywall underneath.

b. Wetting:

- Fill a spray bottle with warm water or your chosen removal solution.
- Spray the surface of the wallpaper liberally, ensuring even coverage.
- Allow the solution to soak into the wallpaper for 10-15 minutes, or according to the product instructions.
- For stubborn wallpaper, you may need to apply multiple rounds of solution and allow for longer soaking times.

5. Scraping and Removing the Wallpaper:

Once the wallpaper has been thoroughly saturated, it's time to start scraping and removing it from the wall.

a. Starting at a Seam:

- Locate a loose seam or corner of the wallpaper and gently lift it with your scraper or putty knife.
- If the wallpaper is strippable or peelable, it should come off easily in large strips.
- For traditional wallpaper, use your scraper to gently scrape the wallpaper away from the wall, working in a downward motion.

b. Scraping Techniques:
- Hold your scraper at a 30-45 degree angle to the wall, applying steady pressure as you scrape.
- Work in small, manageable sections, gradually moving across the wall.
- If you encounter stubborn areas, re-wet them with your removal solution and allow for additional soaking time before attempting to scrape again.

c. Removing Residue:
- After removing the majority of the wallpaper, you may still have some adhesive residue left on the wall.
- To remove this residue, mix equal parts warm water and vinegar in a spray bottle and apply it to the affected areas.
- Allow the solution to sit for several minutes, then scrub the residue with a sponge or scrub brush until it loosens and comes off.

6. Preparing the Wall for New Paint or Wallpaper:

After removing the old wallpaper and residue, it's essential to properly prepare the wall surface before applying new paint or wallpaper.

a. Cleaning the Wall:
- Once all the wallpaper and residue have been removed, wash the wall with a solution of warm water and mild detergent.
- Use a sponge or soft cloth to remove any remaining dirt, dust, or debris.
- Rinse the wall with clean water and allow it to dry completely.

b. Repairing Damage:
- Inspect the wall for any damage, such as cracks, holes, or dents.
- Repair these imperfections using spackling compound or drywall joint compound, following the manufacturer's instructions.
- Sand the repaired areas smooth and wipe away any dust with a clean, damp cloth.

c. Priming:

- Before painting or applying new wallpaper, prime the wall surface to ensure even coverage and proper adhesion.
- Choose a primer suitable for your intended finish (paint or wallpaper) and apply it according to the manufacturer's instructions.
- Allow the primer to dry completely before proceeding with your new wall covering.

Removing old wallpaper can be a labor-intensive process, but with the right tools, techniques, and patience, you can achieve a clean, smooth surface ready for a fresh new look. Remember to work methodically, take breaks as needed, and don't hesitate to enlist the help of friends or family members to make the job more manageable.

If you encounter particularly stubborn wallpaper or extensive damage to the wall surface, it may be best to consult with a professional contractor who has the experience and equipment to handle more challenging removal projects. With the old wallpaper successfully removed and the wall properly prepared, you'll be ready to transform your space with a beautiful new paint job or wallpaper design.

Applying New Wallpaper

Once you've removed the old wallpaper and prepared the wall surface, applying new wallpaper can be an exciting way to transform the look and feel of your space. With a wide variety of colors, patterns, and textures available, wallpaper offers countless design possibilities. In this section, we'll walk you through the process of applying new wallpaper, including the tools, techniques, and tips needed to achieve a professional-looking result.

1. Choosing the Right Wallpaper:

Before beginning the application process, it's important to select the right wallpaper for your space and design goals.

a. Types of Wallpaper:

- Pre-pasted: This type of wallpaper has a pre-applied adhesive that is activated by water, making it easier to install.
- Unpasted: Unpasted wallpaper requires the application of wallpaper paste to the back of each strip before hanging.
- Self-adhesive: Also known as peel-and-stick wallpaper, this type has a removable adhesive backing that allows for easy installation and removal.

b. Patterns and Repeats:

- Consider the scale and style of the pattern you choose, ensuring it complements your room's size and décor.
- Pay attention to the repeat size, which is the vertical distance between where the pattern matches up again. This will affect the amount of wallpaper needed and the placement of each strip.

c. Durability and Cleanability:

- Choose a wallpaper that is appropriate for the room's function and level of use.
- Consider factors such as moisture resistance, light fastness, and washability, especially for high-traffic areas or rooms prone to humidity.

2. Gathering Tools and Materials:

Having the right tools and materials on hand will make the wallpaper application process more efficient and successful.

a. Essential Tools:
- Measuring tape
- Pencil and straightedge
- Scissors and utility knife
- Smoothing brush or plastic smoother
- Seam roller
- Level
- Sponge and bucket

b. Application Materials:
- Wallpaper paste (for unpasted wallpaper)
- Water tray (for pre-pasted wallpaper)
- Drop cloths or plastic sheeting
- Painter's tape

c. Preparation Materials:
- Wall sizing or primer
- Spackling compound or drywall joint compound (for wall repairs)
- Sandpaper (for smoothing repairs)

3. Preparing the Room and Walls:

Before starting the wallpaper application, take steps to protect your floors and furniture and ensure the walls are properly prepared.

a. Protecting the Space:
- Clear the room of furniture, or move it to the center and cover it with drop cloths or plastic sheeting.
- Remove outlet and switch covers, and cover the openings with painter's tape.
- Cover the floor along the base of the wall with drop cloths or plastic sheeting.

b. Cleaning and Repairing Walls:
- Ensure the walls are clean, dry, and free of dust or debris.
- Repair any imperfections, such as cracks or holes, using spackling compound or drywall joint compound, and sand the repairs smooth.

c. Priming or Sizing:
- Apply a wallpaper primer or wall sizing to the prepared walls, following the manufacturer's instructions.
- This step helps to create a smooth, even surface for the wallpaper to adhere to and can make future removal easier.

4. Measuring and Cutting Wallpaper:

Accurate measuring and cutting are crucial for achieving a seamless, professional look.

a. Measuring the Walls:
- Measure the height of your walls, adding a few inches to allow for trimming at the top and bottom.
- Determine the number of strips needed by dividing the room's perimeter by the width of the wallpaper, accounting for pattern repeats.

b. Cutting Strips:
- Cut the first strip of wallpaper to the measured length, adding a few inches for trimming.
- For patterned wallpaper, ensure the pattern is properly aligned before cutting subsequent strips.
- Label each strip in the order it will be hung to avoid confusion.

c. Matching Patterns:
- For wallpaper with a large or complex pattern, consider starting the first strip in the center of a focal wall and working outward to ensure a balanced look.
- Overlap the strips slightly at the seams, making sure the pattern matches precisely before trimming the excess.

5. Applying the Wallpaper:

With the strips cut and the walls prepared, it's time to begin applying the wallpaper.

a. Activating the Adhesive:

- For pre-pasted wallpaper, roll the strip loosely (adhesive side out) and submerge it in a water tray for the recommended time, typically 30 seconds to 1 minute.
- For unpasted wallpaper, apply the paste evenly to the back of the strip using a paint roller or brush.

b. Hanging the First Strip:

- Begin hanging the wallpaper at a corner or a plumb line, ensuring the strip is straight and level.
- Smooth the strip from the center outward using a smoothing brush or plastic smoother, working out any air bubbles or wrinkles.
- Trim excess wallpaper at the top and bottom using a utility knife and straightedge.

c. Hanging Subsequent Strips:

- Align the second strip with the edge of the first, making sure the pattern matches perfectly.
- Smooth the strip as before, using a seam roller to ensure a tight, flat seam between the strips.
- Continue hanging strips in this manner, working around the room and around obstacles like windows and doors.

6. Trimming and Finishing:

After hanging all the wallpaper strips, attend to the details to ensure a polished, professional look.

a. Trimming Edges:

- Use a sharp utility knife and a straightedge to trim any excess wallpaper along the top, bottom, and around obstacles.
- For a clean, precise cut, slightly score the wallpaper first, then follow up with a firm, smooth cut.

b. Smoothing Seams and Edges:
- Run a seam roller over all the seams to ensure they are tight and flat.
- Use a damp sponge to gently clean any excess adhesive from the surface of the wallpaper and surrounding trim.

c. Replacing Fixtures:
- Allow the wallpaper to dry completely, typically 24-48 hours, before replacing outlet and switch covers and moving furniture back into place.
- Gently cut around the edges of outlet and switch openings using a sharp utility knife before replacing the covers.

By following these steps and paying close attention to detail, you can successfully apply new wallpaper and transform the look of your space. Remember to work patiently, double-check measurements and alignments, and don't hesitate to enlist the help of a friend or family member for an extra set of hands.

If you encounter any challenges or are unsure about a particular step in the process, consult the wallpaper manufacturer's instructions or consider seeking the guidance of a professional wallpaper installer. With your newly applied wallpaper in place, you can enjoy a fresh, updated look that reflects your personal style and enhances the overall ambiance of your room.

Chapter 6
Flooring Projects
Installing Laminate and Vinyl Flooring

Laminate and vinyl flooring are popular choices for DIY flooring projects due to their affordability, durability, and ease of installation. Both types of flooring offer a wide range of styles and patterns to suit any décor, from classic wood looks to modern stone or tile designs. In this section, we'll guide you through the process of installing laminate and vinyl flooring, including the tools, techniques, and tips needed to achieve a professional-looking result.

1. Choosing the Right Flooring:

Before beginning the installation process, it's important to select the right laminate or vinyl flooring for your space and needs.

a. Laminate Flooring:

- Laminate is a synthetic flooring product made from layers of compressed wood and resin, topped with a photographic image and a clear protective layer.
- It is durable, scratch-resistant, and easy to clean, making it ideal for high-traffic areas.
- Laminate flooring comes in a wide range of wood and stone looks, and is available in various thicknesses and plank sizes.

b. Vinyl Flooring:

- Vinyl flooring is made from PVC (polyvinyl chloride) and comes in both sheet and tile or plank formats.
- It is water-resistant, making it a great choice for bathrooms, kitchens, and laundry rooms.
- Vinyl flooring offers a wide variety of patterns and textures, including wood, stone, and tile looks.

c. Subfloor Considerations:
- Consider the type and condition of your subfloor when selecting your flooring material.
- Both laminate and vinyl can be installed over most existing floors, such as wood, tile, or vinyl, as long as the surface is clean, flat, and structurally sound.
- For concrete subfloors, ensure the surface is dry and free of moisture issues before installation.

2. Gathering Tools and Materials:

Having the right tools and materials on hand will make the installation process more efficient and successful.

a. Essential Tools:
- Measuring tape and straight edge
- Pencil and utility knife
- Spacers (for maintaining expansion gaps)
- Tapping block and pull bar
- Rubber mallet
- Saw (miter, circular, or jigsaw) for cutting planks or tiles
- Safety glasses and dust mask

b. Additional Materials:
- Underlayment (if required)
- Transition strips and moldings
- Flooring adhesive (for glue-down vinyl installations)
- Cleaning supplies (broom, vacuum, damp cloth)

3. Preparing the Room and Subfloor:

Before starting the installation, take steps to prepare the room and ensure the subfloor is clean, flat, and dry.

a. Clearing the Space:
- Remove all furniture, appliances, and fixtures from the room.
- Remove any existing flooring (if necessary) and dispose of it properly.

b. Cleaning the Subfloor:
- Sweep or vacuum the subfloor to remove any dust, debris, or loose particles.
- If installing over existing flooring, ensure it is securely attached and free of any wax, polish, or sealant.

c. Leveling the Subfloor:
- Check the subfloor for any unevenness, high spots, or low spots.
- Use a self-leveling compound to fill in low spots and create a smooth, even surface.
- Sand down any high spots to ensure a level surface.

d. Addressing Moisture:
- For concrete subfloors, perform a moisture test to ensure the surface is dry.
- If moisture is present, use a moisture barrier or sealant before installing the new flooring.

4. Planning the Layout:

Creating a plan for your flooring layout will help ensure a balanced, professional look and minimize waste.

a. Measuring the Room:
- Measure the length and width of the room, and calculate the total square footage.
- Add an extra 10% to account for cuts and waste.

b. Determining the Layout:
- Decide on the direction you want the planks or tiles to run (typically parallel to the longest wall or the main entrance).
- Consider the placement of seams and transitions, aiming to minimize their visibility.

c. Dry Laying:
- Before installing, lay out a few rows of planks or tiles without adhesive to visualize the layout and make any necessary adjustments.
- This will also help you identify any potential issues or obstacles, such as uneven walls or door frames.

5. Installing the Flooring:

With the room prepared and layout planned, it's time to begin installing the laminate or vinyl flooring.

a. Starting the First Row:

- Begin installing the first row along the longest wall, leaving a 1/4-inch expansion gap between the flooring and the wall.
- Use spacers to maintain this gap and ensure a straight line.

b. Clicking and Locking (Laminate):

- For laminate flooring, connect the planks by inserting the tongue of one plank into the groove of the adjacent plank at a slight angle, then lowering it into place.
- Use a tapping block and rubber mallet to gently tap the planks together for a snug fit.

c. Cutting and Fitting:

- Measure and cut planks or tiles as needed to fit around obstacles or to fill in the end of each row.
- Use a utility knife or saw to make straight cuts, and a jigsaw for more intricate cuts around door frames or pipes.

d. Gluing and Rolling (Vinyl):

- For glue-down vinyl installations, apply the adhesive to the subfloor using a trowel, following the manufacturer's instructions.
- Lay the vinyl planks or tiles into the adhesive, pressing firmly to ensure a good bond.
- Use a floor roller to apply even pressure and remove any air bubbles.

6. Finishing and Maintenance:

After installing the flooring, add the finishing touches and follow proper maintenance procedures to ensure longevity.

a. Installing Moldings and Transitions:

- Install quarter-round or base moldings along the walls to cover the expansion gaps and create a finished look.

- Use transition strips to create a smooth transition between different flooring types or to separate rooms.

b. Cleaning and Protecting:

- Remove any spacers, adhesive residue, or debris from the surface of the flooring.
- Clean the flooring using a soft broom, vacuum, or damp mop, following the manufacturer's recommendations.
- Consider applying a protective sealant or polish to enhance the flooring's durability and resistance to wear and tear.

c. Regular Maintenance:

- Sweep or vacuum the flooring regularly to remove dirt and debris.
- Clean up spills promptly to prevent staining or damage to the flooring.
- Avoid excessive moisture and standing water, which can damage laminate or vinyl flooring over time.
- Use felt pads or protectors under furniture legs to prevent scratches and indentations.

By following these steps and paying attention to the specific requirements of your chosen flooring product, you can successfully install laminate or vinyl flooring in your home. Remember to work patiently, measure carefully, and don't hesitate to consult the manufacturer's instructions or a professional installer if you encounter any challenges or are unsure about a particular step in the process.

With your newly installed laminate or vinyl flooring, you can enjoy a beautiful, durable, and easy-to-maintain surface that enhances the look and functionality of your space for years to come.

Replacing Damaged Tiles

Tile flooring is a popular choice for its durability, easy maintenance, and versatile design options. However, over time, tiles can become damaged due to impact, heavy foot traffic, or settling of the subfloor. Replacing damaged tiles is an important task to maintain the integrity and appearance of your tile floor. In this section, we'll walk you through the process of replacing damaged tiles, including the tools, techniques, and tips needed to achieve a seamless repair.

1. Identifying the Damaged Tile:
The first step in replacing a damaged tile is to assess the extent of the damage and identify the specific tile that needs to be replaced.

a. Types of Damage:
- Cracks: Tiles can develop cracks due to heavy impacts, structural movement, or improper installation.
- Chips: Tiles may chip along the edges or corners, especially in high-traffic areas or around doorways.
- Loose or Hollow Tiles: Tiles that sound hollow when tapped or feel loose underfoot may indicate a problem with the adhesive or subfloor.

b. Matching Replacement Tiles:
- If possible, use a spare tile from the original installation or purchase a matching replacement tile from the same manufacturer and batch.
- If an exact match is not available, consider replacing multiple tiles in a pattern or accent design to create a cohesive look.

2. Gathering Tools and Materials:
Having the right tools and materials on hand will make the tile replacement process more efficient and successful.

a. Essential Tools:
- Safety glasses and work gloves

- Grout saw or utility knife
- Hammer and chisel
- Putty knife or flat pry bar
- Notched trowel
- Rubber float
- Grout sponge and bucket

b. Materials:
- Replacement tile(s)
- Tile adhesive or mortar
- Grout (matching the existing grout color)
- Spacers (if needed)
- Clean cloths or rags

3. Removing the Damaged Tile:

To replace a damaged tile, you must first remove it carefully to avoid damaging surrounding tiles.

a. Removing Grout:
- Using a grout saw or utility knife, carefully cut through the grout around the damaged tile, creating a clear outline.
- Remove as much of the grout as possible to expose the edges of the tile.

b. Loosening the Tile:
- Place the chisel at a 45-degree angle against the center of the damaged tile and gently tap with a hammer to create a small hole or crack.
- Work the chisel around the edges of the tile to loosen it from the adhesive.

c. Prying Out the Tile:
- Insert a putty knife or flat pry bar into the gap created by the chisel and gently pry up the tile, working from the center outward.
- If the tile is stubborn, use a hammer to gently tap the pry bar and apply leverage.

- Remove any remaining pieces of the broken tile and clean out the adhesive from the subfloor using a putty knife.

4. Preparing the Surface:
Before installing the replacement tile, ensure the surface is clean, dry, and level.

a. Cleaning the Area:
- Scrape away any old adhesive or debris from the subfloor using a putty knife.
- Vacuum or sweep the area to remove any dust or small particles.

b. Leveling the Surface:
- Check the subfloor for any unevenness or damage, and repair as needed using a self-leveling compound or patching material.
- Allow any repairs to dry completely before proceeding.

5. Installing the Replacement Tile:
With the surface prepared, you can now install the replacement tile.

a. Applying Adhesive:
- Using a notched trowel, apply a layer of tile adhesive or mortar to the back of the replacement tile, following the manufacturer's instructions.
- Ensure the adhesive is evenly distributed and covers the entire back of the tile.

b. Placing the Tile:
- Carefully place the replacement tile into the empty space, aligning it with the surrounding tiles.
- Use spacers if needed to maintain consistent grout lines.
- Press the tile firmly into place, ensuring it is level with the adjacent tiles.

c. Allowing Adhesive to Set:
- Allow the adhesive to set according to the manufacturer's instructions, typically 24-48 hours.

- Avoid walking on the newly installed tile during this time.

6. Grouting and Finishing:
Once the adhesive has set, you can grout the replacement tile to blend it seamlessly with the surrounding tiles.
a. Mixing the Grout:
- Mix the grout according to the manufacturer's instructions, ensuring a consistent color and texture.
- For small repairs, you may be able to purchase pre-mixed grout for convenience.
b. Applying the Grout:
- Using a rubber float, spread the grout over the joints surrounding the replacement tile, pressing it firmly into the gaps.
- Hold the float at a 45-degree angle and work diagonally across the joints to ensure even coverage.
- Remove excess grout from the tile surface using the float held at a 90-degree angle.
c. Cleaning and Finishing:
- Allow the grout to set for 10-15 minutes, then gently wipe the tile surface with a damp grout sponge to remove any remaining grout haze.
- Be careful not to disturb the grout lines while cleaning.
- Allow the grout to cure for at least 24 hours before walking on the tile or exposing it to moisture.

7. Maintaining and Preventing Future Damage:
To keep your tile flooring looking its best and prevent future damage, follow these maintenance tips:
a. Regular Cleaning:
- Sweep or vacuum your tile floor regularly to remove dirt and debris.
- Mop the floor using a pH-neutral cleaner and warm water, following the manufacturer's instructions.

b. Preventing Damage:
- Place mats or rugs at entrances to capture dirt and moisture before it reaches the tile floor.
- Use felt pads or furniture protectors under heavy furniture to prevent scratches and cracks.
- Avoid dropping heavy objects on the tile floor, which can cause chips or cracks.

c. Sealing Grout:
- Consider applying a grout sealer to protect the grout from stains and moisture.
- Reapply the sealer as needed, following the manufacturer's recommendations.

By following these steps and taking a methodical approach to replacing damaged tiles, you can maintain the beauty and integrity of your tile flooring. Remember to work patiently, use the appropriate tools and materials, and take necessary safety precautions.

If you encounter extensive damage or are unsure about any step in the process, don't hesitate to consult a professional tile installer for guidance or assistance. With proper care and maintenance, your tile flooring can provide a durable and attractive surface for years to come.

Refinishing Hardwood Floors

Hardwood floors are a beautiful and timeless feature in many homes, adding warmth, character, and value to any space. Over time, however, hardwood floors can become worn, scratched, or discolored due to heavy foot traffic, spills, or exposure to sunlight. Refinishing hardwood floors is a cost-effective way to restore their natural beauty and protect them from further damage. In this section, we'll guide you through the process of refinishing hardwood floors, including the tools, techniques, and tips needed to achieve a professional-looking result.

1. Assessing the Floor Condition:
Before beginning the refinishing process, it's essential to assess the condition of your hardwood floors to determine the extent of work required.
  a. Evaluating Wear and Damage:
  - Inspect the floor for signs of wear, such as scratches, dents, or discoloration.
  - Check for any deep gouges or structural damage that may require repair before refinishing.
  b. Testing for Wax or Sealant:
  - In some cases, hardwood floors may have a layer of wax or sealant that must be removed before refinishing.
  - To test for wax, scrape a small area of the floor with a putty knife. If wax buildup is present, it will appear as a grayish-white residue on the blade.
  c. Determining the Sanding Depth:
  - The number of times the floor has been previously sanded will impact the depth of sanding required.
  - Floors that have been sanded multiple times may have a thinner wear layer, limiting the number of future refinishing options.

2. Gathering Tools and Materials:

Having the right tools and materials on hand will make the refinishing process more efficient and successful.

a. Essential Tools:
- Safety gear (dust mask, goggles, ear protection)
- Drum sander or orbital sander
- Edge sander
- Palm sander or detail sander
- Sanding belts and pads (various grits)
- Vacuum cleaner with HEPA filter
- Putty knife and wood filler
- Paint roller and tray
- Natural-bristle brush

b. Materials:
- Stain (optional)
- Wood conditioner (for even stain application)
- Polyurethane sealer (oil-based or water-based)
- Mineral spirits (for cleaning and thinning oil-based products)
- Tack cloths
- Sandpaper (various grits)

3. Preparing the Room:

Before sanding, take steps to prepare the room and protect yourself and your belongings from dust and debris.

a. Clearing the Space:
- Remove all furniture, rugs, and window coverings from the room.
- Cover any remaining fixtures or built-ins with plastic sheeting and tape.

b. Sealing Off the Area:
- Close and seal any doors leading to other rooms to prevent dust from spreading throughout the house.
- Cover air vents and electrical outlets with plastic sheeting and tape.

c. Ensuring Proper Ventilation:
- Open windows to allow for adequate ventilation during sanding and finishing.
- Use fans to help circulate air and remove dust from the room.

4. Sanding the Floor:

Sanding is the most critical step in the refinishing process, as it removes the old finish, smooths the surface, and prepares the wood for staining and sealing.

a. Rough Sanding:
- Begin with a coarse-grit sandpaper (20-40 grit) on the drum sander to remove the old finish and level the floor.
- Work in the direction of the wood grain, overlapping each pass slightly to ensure even sanding.
- Use an edge sander to sand along the perimeter of the room and in hard-to-reach areas.

b. Medium Sanding:
- Switch to a medium-grit sandpaper (50-80 grit) to remove scratches from the rough sanding and further smooth the surface.
- Continue sanding with the grain, using the same technique as before.

c. Fine Sanding:
- Finish with a fine-grit sandpaper (100-120 grit) to achieve a smooth, even surface ready for staining and sealing.
- Use a palm sander or detail sander for corners, edges, and hard-to-reach areas.

d. Cleaning and Filling:
- Vacuum the floor thoroughly to remove all dust and debris.
- Fill any cracks, holes, or imperfections with wood filler, following the manufacturer's instructions.
- Allow the filler to dry completely, then sand the filled areas smooth with fine-grit sandpaper.

5. Staining the Floor (Optional):

If you want to change the color of your hardwood floor, staining is an optional step before sealing.

a. Choosing a Stain:

- Select a wood stain that complements your décor and the natural color of your hardwood.
- Consider the undertones of the wood and how they will interact with the stain color.

b. Applying Wood Conditioner:

- To ensure even stain absorption, apply a wood conditioner to the floor before staining
- Follow the manufacturer's instructions for application and drying time.

c. Applying the Stain:

- Using a natural-bristle brush or a rag, apply the stain evenly to the floor, working with the grain.
- Wipe away excess stain with a clean cloth, ensuring an even application.
- Allow the stain to dry completely, following the manufacturer's recommended drying time.

6. Sealing the Floor:

Sealing the floor protects the wood from moisture, wear, and damage while enhancing its natural beauty.

a. Choosing a Sealer:

- Select a polyurethane sealer appropriate for your floor's use and desired finish (glossy, semi-gloss, or satin).
- Choose between oil-based and water-based sealers, considering factors such as durability, drying time, and odor.

b. Applying the Sealer:

- Using a paint roller or natural-bristle brush, apply a thin, even coat of sealer to the floor, following the grain.
- Avoid overworking the sealer, which can cause bubbles or brush marks.

- Allow the first coat to dry completely, then lightly sand with fine-grit sandpaper (220-grit) to remove any imperfections.

c. Applying Additional Coats:

- Apply a second coat of sealer, following the same technique as the first coat.
- For maximum durability, consider applying a third coat, especially in high-traffic areas.
- Allow the final coat to dry completely, typically 24-48 hours, before replacing furniture and rugs.

7. Maintaining Refinished Hardwood Floors:

To keep your newly refinished hardwood floors looking beautiful for years to come, follow these maintenance tips:

a. Regular Cleaning:

- Sweep, dust, or vacuum your floors regularly to remove dirt and debris.
- Use a slightly damp mop or cloth to clean the floors, avoiding excessive moisture.

b. Protecting the Finish:

- Place mats or rugs at entrances to capture dirt and moisture before it reaches the hardwood.
- Use felt pads or furniture protectors under heavy furniture to prevent scratches and dents.
- Avoid walking on the floors with high heels or sports cleats, which can damage the finish.

c. Addressing Wear and Tear:

- Periodically inspect the floors for signs of wear or damage, such as scratches or dullness.
- Use touch-up kits or spot-refinishing techniques to address minor imperfections and extend the life of the finish.

By following these steps and taking a meticulous approach to refinishing your hardwood floors, you can restore their natural beauty and protect them for years to come. Remember to work patiently, use the appropriate tools and materials, and prioritize safety throughout the process.

If you encounter extensive damage or are unsure about any step in the refinishing process, consider consulting a professional flooring contractor for guidance or assistance. With proper care and maintenance, your refinished hardwood floors will provide a stunning and durable foundation for your home's décor.

Laying Wall-to-Wall Carpet

Wall-to-wall carpeting is a popular flooring choice that offers comfort, insulation, and a wide range of design options. Installing wall-to-wall carpet can be a challenging DIY project, but with the right tools, techniques, and preparation, you can achieve a professional-looking result. In this section, we'll guide you through the process of laying wall-to-wall carpet, including the tools, materials, and steps needed for a successful installation.

1. Measuring the Room:

Accurate measurements are essential for ordering the correct amount of carpet and ensuring a proper fit.

a. Room Dimensions:

- Measure the length and width of the room, recording the longest measurements in each direction.
- For irregular-shaped rooms, divide the space into smaller rectangles, measure each section, and add the measurements together.

b. Calculating Carpet Quantity:

- Multiply the length by the width to determine the total square footage of the room.
- Add an extra 10% to account for waste, cuts, and seams.
- Consult with your carpet supplier to ensure you order the appropriate amount based on the carpet width and dye lot.

2. Gathering Tools and Materials:

Having the right tools and materials on hand will make the installation process more efficient and successful.

a. Tools:

- Tape measure
- Chalk line
- Carpet knife or utility knife
- Carpet stretcher or power stretcher
- Knee kicker

- Carpet seam roller
- Hammer
- Staple gun
- Carpenter's square

b. Materials:

- Carpet padding
- Tack strips
- Carpet seam tape
- Carpet adhesive
- Threshold bars or transition strips
- Staples
- Nails

3. Preparing the Subfloor:

Before installing the carpet, ensure the subfloor is clean, dry, and level.

a. Removing Old Flooring:

- Remove any existing flooring, such as old carpet, padding, or tack strips.
- Dispose of the old materials properly, following local regulations.

b. Cleaning the Subfloor:

- Sweep or vacuum the subfloor to remove any dirt, debris, or loose particles.
- If necessary, use a scraper to remove any adhesive residue or stubborn debris.

c. Addressing Subfloor Issues:

- Inspect the subfloor for any damage, unevenness, or squeaks.
- Repair any cracks, holes, or weak spots with a suitable patching compound or wood filler.
- Use a self-leveling compound to address any significant unevenness in the subfloor.

4. Installing Tack Strips and Padding:

Tack strips and padding provide a foundation for the carpet and enhance its comfort and durability.

a. Attaching Tack Strips:
- Place tack strips around the perimeter of the room, about 1/2 inch from the walls.
- Ensure the tacks are facing toward the wall and the strips are securely nailed or stapled in place.

b. Fitting the Padding:
- Cut the carpet padding to fit the room, allowing for a slight overlap onto the tack strips.
- Staple the padding to the subfloor, using a staple gun and following the manufacturer's recommendations for staple spacing.

c. Sealing Seams:
- Use carpet seam tape to seal any seams in the padding, ensuring a smooth and continuous surface.

5. Laying and Cutting the Carpet:

With the padding in place, you can now lay and cut the carpet to fit the room.

a. Positioning the Carpet:
- Place the carpet in the room, allowing an extra 4-6 inches on each side for trimming.
- Ensure the carpet pile is running in the desired direction and the seams (if any) are in the least noticeable areas.

b. Cutting the Carpet:
- Use a carpet knife or utility knife to trim the excess carpet along the walls, leaving about 1/2 inch of excess for tucking.
- Make relief cuts around any obstacles, such as doorways or floor vents, to allow the carpet to lay flat.

c. Seaming the Carpet (if necessary):
- If the room requires multiple pieces of carpet, join them using carpet seam tape and a seam roller.

- Follow the manufacturer's instructions for activating the adhesive on the seam tape and pressing the carpet edges together.

6. Stretching and Securing the Carpet:
Stretching the carpet ensures a taut, wrinkle-free surface and helps prevent future sagging or buckling.

a. Using a Knee Kicker:
- Start in one corner of the room and use a knee kicker to hook the carpet onto the tack strip.
- Work your way along the wall, stretching the carpet and securing it to the tack strip with the knee kicker.

b. Using a Power Stretcher:
- For larger rooms or more stubborn wrinkles, use a power stretcher to achieve a tighter stretch.
- Place the power stretcher in the center of the room and stretch the carpet toward the walls, securing it to the tack strips.

c. Trimming and Tucking:
- After stretching, trim any excess carpet along the walls, leaving about 1/2 inch for tucking.
- Use a carpeting chisel or stair tool to tuck the excess carpet into the gap between the tack strip and the wall.

7. Installing Threshold Bars and Transitions:
To create a clean and finished look, install threshold bars or transition strips where the carpet meets other flooring types or doorways.

a. Choosing the Right Transition:
- Select a threshold bar or transition strip that matches the height and style of your carpet and the adjacent flooring.
- Ensure the transition allows for a smooth and safe passage between the different flooring surfaces.

b. Cutting and Fitting:
- Measure and cut the threshold bar or transition strip to fit the doorway or flooring edge.

- If necessary, use a hacksaw or miter saw to make precise cuts and angles.

c. Securing the Transition:

- Attach the threshold bar or transition strip to the subfloor using the appropriate fasteners, such as screws or adhesive.
- Ensure the transition is level and securely in place to prevent tripping hazards.

8. Maintaining Your Carpet:

To keep your newly installed carpet looking and feeling its best, follow these maintenance tips:

a. Vacuuming:

- Vacuum your carpet regularly, using a high-quality vacuum cleaner with adjustable height settings.
- Pay extra attention to high-traffic areas and use slow, overlapping strokes to remove dirt and debris.

b. Stain Removal:

- Address spills and stains promptly, blotting the area with a clean, damp cloth or following the carpet manufacturer's recommended cleaning methods.
- For tough stains, use a carpet-specific cleaning solution or consult a professional carpet cleaning service.

c. Professional Cleaning:

- Schedule professional deep cleaning for your carpet every 12-18 months, or more frequently in high-traffic areas.
- A professional cleaning will help remove embedded dirt, restore the carpet pile, and extend the life of your carpet.

By following these steps and taking a careful, methodical approach to laying wall-to-wall carpet, you can achieve a beautiful and long-lasting flooring solution for your home. Remember to measure accurately, use the appropriate tools and materials, and take your time to ensure a professional-looking result.

If you encounter any challenges or are unsure about any part of the installation process, don't hesitate to consult a professional carpet installer for guidance or assistance. With proper installation and maintenance, your wall-to-wall carpet will provide comfort, style, and durability for years to come.

Creating a Tiled Backsplash

A tiled backsplash is a stylish and functional addition to any kitchen or bathroom, protecting the walls from moisture and splashes while adding visual interest and character to the space. Installing a tiled backsplash is a rewarding DIY project that can be completed in a weekend with the right tools, materials, and techniques. In this section, we'll guide you through the process of creating a tiled backsplash, including the steps for planning, preparation, installation, and finishing.

1. Planning Your Backsplash Design:
   Before beginning the installation process, take time to plan your backsplash design and layout.
   a. Choosing Tiles:
   - Select tiles that complement your kitchen or bathroom's style, color scheme, and existing finishes.
   - Consider factors such as tile size, material, pattern, and texture when making your choice.
   - Order a sample tile to see how it looks in your space before committing to a full order.
   b. Determining Layout:
   - Decide on the placement and arrangement of your tiles, taking into account any outlets, switches, or appliances that will interrupt the layout.
   - Create a scale drawing of your backsplash design, including measurements and tile placement, to use as a guide during installation.
   c. Calculating Tile Quantity:
   - Measure the width and height of the backsplash area, subtracting any appliances or fixtures.
   - Calculate the square footage by multiplying the width by the height.
   - Add an extra 10% to account for cuts, waste, and potential breakage.

2. Gathering Tools and Materials:

Having the right tools and materials on hand will make the installation process more efficient and successful.

a. Tools:
- Tile cutter or wet saw
- Tile nippers
- Notched trowel
- Grout float
- Rubber grout sponge
- Bucket
- Measuring tape
- Level
- Pencil
- Drill with mixing attachment (for mixing thinset)

b. Materials:
- Tiles
- Thinset mortar
- Grout
- Spacers
- Caulk
- Backing material (if needed)
- Drop cloth or protective sheeting

3. Preparing the Wall Surface:

Before installing the tiles, ensure the wall surface is clean, dry, and properly prepared.

a. Cleaning:
- Remove any existing wallpaper, paint, or debris from the wall surface.
- Clean the wall with a degreaser or all-purpose cleaner to remove any grease, grime, or residue.

b. Repairing:
- Repair any cracks, holes, or imperfections in the wall surface using spackling compound or drywall joint compound.

- Sand the repaired areas smooth and wipe away any dust with a damp cloth.

c. Priming (if necessary):

- If the wall surface is painted or glossy, apply a bonding primer to ensure proper adhesion of the thinset mortar.
- Allow the primer to dry completely before proceeding with the installation.

4. Installing the Tiles:

With the wall surface prepared, you can now begin installing the tiles according to your planned design.

a. Applying Thinset Mortar:

- Mix the thinset mortar according to the manufacturer's instructions, using a drill with a mixing attachment.
- Apply the thinset to the wall using a notched trowel, covering an area of approximately 3-4 square feet at a time.
- Comb the thinset in one direction using the notched edge of the trowel, creating ridges for the tiles to adhere to.

b. Setting the Tiles:

- Begin setting the tiles in place, starting at the center of the backsplash and working outward.
- Use spacers between the tiles to ensure consistent gaps for grouting.
- Press each tile firmly into the thinset, using a slight twisting motion to ensure good contact and adhesion.
- Check the tiles periodically with a level to maintain a consistent and even surface.

c. Cutting Tiles (if necessary):

- Use a tile cutter or wet saw to make straight cuts on tiles as needed to fit around outlets, switches, or at the edges of the backsplash.
- For more intricate cuts or curves, use tile nippers to carefully remove small pieces of tile until the desired shape is achieved.

d. Allowing Thinset to Cure:
- Once all tiles are in place, allow the thinset mortar to cure according to the manufacturer's instructions, typically 24-48 hours.
- Avoid disturbing the tiles during this curing period to ensure proper adhesion.

5. Grouting and Finishing:

After the thinset has cured, you can grout the tiles and add finishing touches to your backsplash.

a. Mixing and Applying Grout:
- Mix the grout according to the manufacturer's instructions, using a drill with a mixing attachment.
- Remove the spacers from between the tiles and apply the grout using a grout float, holding it at a 45-degree angle to the tile surface.
- Work the grout into the gaps between the tiles, ensuring complete coverage and removing any excess grout from the tile surface.

b. Cleaning Tiles:
- Allow the grout to set for 10-15 minutes, then wipe the tile surface with a damp grout sponge to remove any remaining grout haze.
- Be careful not to remove too much grout from the joints, maintaining a consistent depth and appearance.
- Allow the grout to cure for 24-48 hours before cleaning the tiles with a pH-neutral cleaner and soft cloth.

c. Sealing Grout (optional):
- To protect the grout from stains and moisture, consider applying a grout sealer according to the manufacturer's instructions.
- Apply the sealer with a brush or sponge, wiping away any excess and allowing it to dry completely.

d. Caulking:
- Apply a bead of caulk along the edges of the backsplash where it meets the countertop, wall, or any other surfaces.
- Smooth the caulk with a wet finger or caulking tool, creating a neat and finished appearance.
- Allow the caulk to dry completely before exposing the backsplash to moisture or use.

6. Maintaining Your Tiled Backsplash:

To keep your newly installed backsplash looking its best, follow these maintenance tips:

a. Regular Cleaning:
- Wipe down the backsplash regularly with a soft cloth or sponge and a pH-neutral cleaner to remove any grease, grime, or splashes.
- Avoid using abrasive cleaners or scrubbers that can scratch or dull the tile surface.

b. Inspecting Grout:
- Periodically inspect the grout for any signs of cracking, chipping, or discoloration.
- Address any damaged or stained grout promptly by cleaning, repairing, or replacing it as necessary.

c. Sealing Grout (if applicable):
- If you have sealed your grout, reapply the sealer every 1-2 years, or as recommended by the manufacturer, to maintain its protective properties.

By following these steps and taking a careful, methodical approach to creating your tiled backsplash, you can achieve a beautiful and long-lasting addition to your kitchen or bathroom. Remember to plan your design carefully, use the appropriate tools and materials, and take your time to ensure a professional-looking result.

If you encounter any challenges or are unsure about any part of the installation process, don't hesitate to consult a professional tile installer for guidance or assistance. With proper installation and maintenance, your tiled backsplash will provide both function and style for years to come, enhancing the overall look and value of your space.

Chapter 7
Outdoor Improvements
Building a Raised Garden Bed

A raised garden bed is an excellent way to enhance your outdoor space while providing a convenient and efficient area for growing plants, vegetables, or herbs. Raised beds offer several advantages over traditional in-ground gardens, such as better soil control, improved drainage, and easier access for planting and maintenance. In this section, we'll guide you through the process of building a raised garden bed, including the materials, tools, and steps needed for a successful project.

1. Planning Your Raised Garden Bed:
   Before starting the construction process, take time to plan the size, location, and design of your raised bed.
   a. Size and Location:
   - Determine the desired size of your raised bed based on the available space and the types of plants you want to grow.
   - Consider factors such as sunlight exposure, proximity to water sources, and accessibility when choosing the location for your bed.
   b. Materials:
   - Select the materials for your raised bed, such as wood (e.g., cedar, redwood, or pressure-treated lumber), stone, or concrete blocks.
   - Consider the durability, aesthetics, and cost of the materials when making your choice.
   c. Design:
   - Decide on the height of your raised bed, typically between 6 and 18 inches, depending on the plants you want to grow and your personal preferences.
   - Consider adding features such as built-in seating, trellises, or irrigation systems to enhance the functionality and appearance of your raised bed.

2. Gathering Tools and Materials:

Having the right tools and materials on hand will make the construction process more efficient and successful.

a. Tools:
- Measuring tape
- Carpenter's square
- Level
- Shovel or spade
- Drill with bits
- Saw (hand saw or circular saw)
- Hammer
- Safety glasses and work gloves

b. Materials:
- Lumber or chosen materials for the bed frame
- Screws or nails
- Landscape fabric (optional)
- Compost or high-quality garden soil
- Gravel or crushed stone (for drainage)

3. Preparing the Site:

Before constructing your raised bed, prepare the site to ensure proper drainage and a level foundation.

a. Clearing the Area:
- Remove any grass, weeds, or debris from the chosen location.
- Use a shovel or spade to level the ground as much as possible.

b. Improving Drainage (optional):
- If your site has poor drainage, consider removing a layer of soil and adding a layer of gravel or crushed stone before building the raised bed.
- This step will help prevent water from pooling and promote better drainage for your plants.

c. Marking the Outline:
- Use measuring tape and a carpenter's square to mark the outline of your raised bed on the ground.

- Drive stakes into the corners of the outline to help guide the placement of your bed frame.

4. Constructing the Frame:
With the site prepared, you can now build the frame for your raised garden bed.

a. Cutting the Lumber:
- Measure and cut the lumber or chosen materials to the desired lengths for your bed frame.
- Use a saw to make straight, clean cuts, ensuring that the edges are square.

b. Assembling the Frame:
- Arrange the cut pieces to form the frame of your raised bed, ensuring that the corners are square and the sides are level.
- Use a drill to pre-drill pilot holes for screws or nails to prevent splitting the wood.
- Secure the frame pieces together with screws or nails, checking for level and making adjustments as needed.

c. Adding Additional Support (optional):
- For larger or taller raised beds, consider adding cross supports or braces to reinforce the frame and prevent bowing or warping over time.
- Use additional lumber or metal brackets to create supportive structures within the frame.

5. Installing Landscape Fabric (optional):
To prevent weeds from growing up through your raised bed and to maintain soil quality, you may choose to install landscape fabric at the bottom of your bed.

a. Measuring and Cutting:
- Measure the interior dimensions of your raised bed frame.
- Cut a piece of landscape fabric slightly larger than the measured dimensions to allow for overlap and secure attachment.

b. Securing the Fabric:
- Place the cut landscape fabric at the bottom of the raised bed frame, ensuring it lays flat and covers the entire surface.
- Secure the fabric to the frame using staples, nails, or landscape pins, pulling it taut to avoid sagging.

c. Creating Drainage Holes:
- Use a utility knife or scissors to cut small holes or slits in the landscape fabric to allow for proper drainage.
- Space the holes evenly across the surface of the fabric to ensure consistent drainage throughout the bed.

6. Filling the Raised Bed:

With the frame constructed and the landscape fabric installed (if desired), you can now fill your raised bed with high-quality soil and compost.

a. Adding Drainage Material (optional):
- If you did not add a layer of gravel or crushed stone during site preparation, consider adding a 1-2 inch layer at the bottom of the bed for improved drainage.

b. Mixing Soil and Compost:
- In a large container or wheelbarrow, mix equal parts high-quality garden soil and well-decomposed compost.
- Blend the soil and compost thoroughly to create a nutrient-rich growing medium for your plants.

c. Filling the Bed:
- Transfer the soil mixture into the raised bed frame, filling it to the desired level (typically 1-2 inches below the top of the frame).
- Use a rake or hoe to level the soil surface and remove any clumps or debris.

7. Planting and Maintaining Your Raised Garden Bed:

With your raised bed constructed and filled, you can now plant your desired crops and maintain the bed for optimal growth.

a. Choosing Plants:

- Select plants, vegetables, or herbs that are well-suited to your climate, sunlight exposure, and the size of your raised bed.
- Consider factors such as plant spacing, mature size, and companion planting when choosing your crops.

b. Planting Techniques:

- Follow the recommended planting depths and spacing for each type of plant or seed.
- Use a trowel or your hands to create planting holes, gently placing the plants or seeds and covering them with soil.
- Water the newly planted bed thoroughly to help settle the soil and promote good root-to-soil contact.

c. Ongoing Maintenance:

- Water your raised bed regularly, keeping the soil consistently moist but not waterlogged.
- Apply a layer of organic mulch (e.g., straw, leaves, or wood chips) to retain moisture, suppress weeds, and regulate soil temperature.
- Monitor your plants for signs of pests, diseases, or nutrient deficiencies, and address any issues promptly using appropriate organic or chemical controls.

By following these steps and taking a thoughtful approach to planning, constructing, and maintaining your raised garden bed, you can create a beautiful and productive growing space in your outdoor area. Remember to choose high-quality materials, take your time during construction, and provide your plants with the care and attention they need to thrive.

If you encounter any challenges or are unsure about any part of the process, don't hesitate to consult experienced gardeners, local garden centers, or online resources for guidance and support. With a well-built and properly maintained raised garden bed, you can enjoy the benefits of fresh, homegrown produce and the satisfaction of creating a thriving green space in your own backyard.

Installing a Paver Patio

A paver patio is an attractive and durable addition to any outdoor living space, providing a stable and stylish surface for entertaining, relaxing, or enjoying your garden. Installing a paver patio is a rewarding DIY project that can be completed with the right tools, materials, and techniques. In this section, we'll guide you through the process of installing a paver patio, including the steps for planning, preparation, installation, and finishing.

1. Planning Your Paver Patio:

Before beginning the installation process, take time to plan the size, location, and design of your paver patio.

a. Size and Location:

- Determine the desired size of your patio based on the available space and your intended use.
- Consider factors such as accessibility, privacy, and the relationship to other outdoor features when choosing the location for your patio.

b. Paver Selection:

- Choose the type and style of pavers that complement your home's architecture and personal preferences.
- Consider factors such as color, texture, shape, and size when making your selection.

c. Design:

- Create a sketch or use design software to plan the layout and pattern of your paver patio.
- Consider incorporating features such as borders, inlays, or curved edges to enhance the visual interest of your patio.

2. Gathering Tools and Materials:

Having the right tools and materials on hand will make the installation process more efficient and successful.

a. Tools:

- Measuring tape

- Shovel
- Level
- Rake
- Rubber mallet
- Plate compactor
- Safety glasses and work gloves

b. Materials:

- Pavers
- Paver base material (e.g., gravel or crushed stone)
- Paver sand
- Edging material (e.g., plastic or metal edging)
- Landscape fabric
- Drainage pipe (if necessary)

3. Preparing the Site:

Before installing your paver patio, prepare the site to ensure proper drainage and a stable foundation.

a. Marking the Area:

- Use measuring tape and stakes to mark the outline of your patio on the ground.
- Use a string or spray paint to create a clear boundary for excavation.

b. Excavating:

- Remove any grass, weeds, or debris from the marked area.
- Excavate the area to a depth of 6-8 inches, depending on the thickness of your pavers and the desired height of your patio.

c. Grading and Compacting:

- Grade the excavated area to ensure proper drainage, sloping the soil away from your home's foundation.
- Use a plate compactor to compact the soil, creating a stable base for your paver patio.

4. Installing the Paver Base:

With the site prepared, you can now install the base material for your paver patio.

a. Laying Landscape Fabric:
- Place landscape fabric over the compacted soil to prevent weed growth and improve drainage.
- Overlap the edges of the fabric by several inches and secure them with landscape staples.

b. Adding Base Material:
- Spread a layer of paver base material (e.g., gravel or crushed stone) over the landscape fabric, maintaining a consistent depth of 4-6 inches.
- Use a rake to level the base material, ensuring a smooth and even surface.

c. Compacting the Base:
- Use a plate compactor to compact the base material, creating a solid foundation for your pavers.
- Make several passes with the compactor to ensure thorough compaction.

5. Laying the Pavers:

With the base installed, you can now begin laying your pavers according to your planned design.

a. Starting the First Row:
- Begin laying pavers along the longest straight edge of your patio, using a string line to ensure a straight and even course.
- Place the pavers tightly together, using a rubber mallet to tap them into place and create a consistent surface.

b. Continuing the Pattern:
- Continue laying pavers in the chosen pattern, working from the straight edge towards the opposite side of the patio.
- Use a level to check the surface of the pavers frequently, making adjustments as needed to maintain a flat and even surface.

c. Cutting Pavers (if necessary):
- For pavers that require cutting to fit along edges or around obstacles, use a masonry saw or paver splitter to make clean, accurate cuts.
- Wear safety glasses and follow the manufacturer's instructions when using cutting tools.

6. Installing Edging and Filling Joints:
After laying the pavers, install edging and fill the joints to secure and finish your patio.

a. Installing Edging:
- Place edging material (e.g., plastic or metal edging) along the perimeter of the patio to hold the pavers in place and prevent shifting.
- Secure the edging with stakes or spikes, following the manufacturer's instructions.

b. Filling Joints with Sand:
- Spread paver sand over the surface of the patio, using a push broom to work the sand into the joints between the pavers.
- Continue adding sand and sweeping until the joints are completely filled and the surface is level.

c. Compacting the Pavers:
- Use a plate compactor to compact the pavers and sand, ensuring a tight and stable surface.
- Make several passes with the compactor, adding more sand to the joints as needed to maintain a consistent fill.

7. Finishing and Maintaining Your Paver Patio:
With the pavers installed and the joints filled, you can now add finishing touches and maintain your patio for long-lasting beauty and durability.

a. Sealing (optional):
- Consider applying a paver sealer to protect your pavers from stains, weathering, and fading.

- Follow the manufacturer's instructions for application and drying times.

b. Cleaning:
- Regularly sweep your paver patio to remove dirt, leaves, and debris.
- For deeper cleaning, use a pressure washer or a paver cleaner, following the manufacturer's instructions.

c. Weed Control:
- Remove any weeds that may grow between the pavers promptly to prevent spreading.
- Apply a granular weed preventer or use a natural solution (e.g., vinegar or boiling water) to discourage weed growth.

By following these steps and taking a careful, methodical approach to installing your paver patio, you can create a beautiful and long-lasting outdoor living space. Remember to plan your design carefully, use high-quality materials, and take your time to ensure a professional-looking result.

If you encounter any challenges or are unsure about any part of the installation process, don't hesitate to consult a professional landscaper or hardscape contractor for guidance or assistance. With proper installation and maintenance, your paver patio will provide years of enjoyment and enhance the overall beauty and functionality of your outdoor area.

Repairing and Sealing a Deck

A well-maintained deck is an inviting and functional outdoor living space that can add value to your home. However, over time, decks can suffer from wear and tear, exposure to the elements, and general deterioration. Regularly repairing and sealing your deck is essential to ensure its longevity, safety, and aesthetic appeal. In this section, we'll guide you through the process of repairing and sealing a deck, including the steps for inspection, cleaning, repair, and sealing.

1. Inspecting Your Deck:

Before beginning any repair or sealing work, thoroughly inspect your deck to identify areas that need attention.

   a. Structural Integrity:
- Check the deck's support posts, beams, and joists for signs of rot, insect damage, or instability.
- Look for any sagging, bouncing, or unevenness in the deck surface, which may indicate underlying structural issues.

   b. Deck Boards:
- Inspect individual deck boards for cracks, splits, warping, or loose nails/screws.
- Note any boards that are severely damaged or rotted and may need to be replaced.

   c. Railings and Stairs:
- Examine railings and stairs for any loose, missing, or damaged components.
- Ensure that railings are securely attached and meet local building codes for height and spacing.

2. Cleaning the Deck:

Before making any repairs or applying sealer, clean your deck thoroughly to remove dirt, grime, and old finishes.

a. Sweeping and Debris Removal:

- Use a broom or leaf blower to remove any loose debris, leaves, or dirt from the deck surface.
- Pay special attention to corners and crevices where debris may accumulate.

b. Pressure Washing:

- Use a pressure washer to remove stubborn dirt, stains, and old finishes from the deck boards.
- Be cautious when using a pressure washer, as excessive pressure can damage the wood fibers.
- Hold the nozzle at a consistent distance and keep it moving to avoid concentrating too much pressure in one spot.

c. Cleaning Solutions:

- For tough stains or mildew, consider using a specialized deck cleaning solution according to the manufacturer's instructions.
- Alternatively, create a homemade cleaning solution using warm water, mild dish soap, and a small amount of bleach.

3. Repairing Deck Components:

After cleaning the deck, address any identified issues to ensure the deck's safety and longevity.

a. Structural Repairs:

- If you noticed any structural issues during the inspection, such as rotted support posts or beams, consult a professional carpenter or contractor for proper repair or replacement.
- Ensure that all structural components are sound and securely connected before proceeding with other repairs.

b. Deck Board Repairs:

- Replace any severely damaged or rotted deck boards with new ones, matching the size and material of the existing boards.

- For minor cracks or splits, use a wood filler or epoxy to fill the voids and sand the area smooth once dry.
- Secure any loose nails or screws, or replace them with new hardware if necessary.

c. Railing and Stair Repairs:

- Tighten or replace any loose or missing railing components, such as balusters or handrails.
- Ensure that stairs are stable and have proper treads and risers, replacing any damaged or rotted components as needed.

4. Sanding and Surface Preparation:

Before applying sealer, prepare the deck surface to ensure proper adhesion and a smooth finish.

a. Sanding:

- Use a belt sander or orbital sander to remove any remaining old finishes, splinters, or rough spots on the deck boards.
- Start with a coarse-grit sandpaper (60-80 grit) and progress to a finer grit (120-150 grit) for a smoother finish.

b. Dust Removal:

- After sanding, use a leaf blower or vacuum to remove any sanding dust from the deck surface and gaps between boards.
- Wipe the surface with a clean, dry cloth to ensure it is free of dust and debris before sealing.

5. Applying Deck Sealer:

Sealing your deck protects the wood from moisture, UV rays, and general wear and tear, extending its lifespan and maintaining its appearance.

a. Choosing a Sealer:

- Select a high-quality deck sealer that is appropriate for your deck's wood type and desired finish (clear, tinted, or semi-transparent).
- Consider factors such as durability, water resistance, and ease of application when choosing a sealer.

b. Application Method:
- Apply the sealer using a brush, roller, or sprayer, following the manufacturer's instructions for the best results.
- Start by applying the sealer to the deck boards, working in the direction of the wood grain and ensuring even coverage.
- Use a brush to apply sealer to hard-to-reach areas, such as gaps between boards or around railings and posts.

c. Multiple Coats:
- Allow the first coat of sealer to dry completely, following the manufacturer's recommended drying time.
- Apply a second coat of sealer, if necessary, to achieve the desired level of protection and finish.

6. Maintaining Your Deck:

Regular maintenance is crucial to keep your deck looking its best and to extend the life of the repairs and sealer.

a. Regular Cleaning:
- Sweep your deck regularly to remove dirt, leaves, and debris.
- Clean your deck annually or as needed using a mild cleaning solution and a soft-bristled brush.

b. Inspections:
- Perform annual inspections of your deck to identify any new issues or areas that may require attention.
- Address any problems promptly to prevent them from escalating into more serious and costly repairs.

c. Re-Sealing:
- Re-apply deck sealer every 1-3 years, depending on the sealer type and the deck's exposure to the elements.
- Before re-sealing, clean and prepare the deck surface as described in the previous steps.

By following these steps and maintaining a regular repair and sealing schedule, you can ensure that your deck remains a safe, attractive, and functional outdoor living space for years to come. Remember to prioritize safety, use high-quality materials, and take your time to achieve the best possible results.

If you encounter any challenges or are unsure about any part of the repair or sealing process, don't hesitate to consult a professional deck contractor or carpenter for guidance or assistance. With proper care and maintenance, your deck will continue to be a valuable and enjoyable addition to your home.

Replacing a Mailbox and House Numbers

A mailbox and house numbers are essential elements of your home's exterior, serving both functional and aesthetic purposes. A well-maintained mailbox ensures that your mail is delivered safely and securely, while clear and visible house numbers help visitors, emergency services, and delivery personnel locate your home easily. Over time, mailboxes and house numbers can become worn, damaged, or outdated, making it necessary to replace them. In this section, we'll guide you through the process of replacing a mailbox and house numbers, including the steps for selecting materials, removing old components, and installing new ones.

1. Choosing a New Mailbox and House Numbers:
   Before beginning the replacement process, select a new mailbox and house numbers that complement your home's style and meet your functional needs.
   a. Mailbox:
   - Consider factors such as size, material (e.g., metal, plastic, or wood), and design when selecting a new mailbox.
   - Ensure that the mailbox conforms to your local post office's guidelines for size and placement.
   - Choose a mailbox that is durable, weather-resistant, and able to accommodate your typical mail volume.
   b. House Numbers:
   - Select house numbers that are clearly visible and easy to read from the street.
   - Consider the material (e.g., metal, plastic, or wood), size, and style of the numbers, ensuring they complement your home's exterior design.
   - Opt for numbers with a contrasting color to your home's exterior to increase visibility.

2. Gathering Tools and Materials:

Having the right tools and materials on hand will make the replacement process more efficient and successful.

a. Tools:

- Screwdriver or drill (depending on the type of fasteners used)
- Wrench or pliers (for removing and attaching bolts or screws)
- Level
- Shovel or post hole digger (if installing a new mailbox post)
- Hammer
- Measuring tape
- Safety goggles and work gloves

b. Materials:

- New mailbox and mounting hardware
- New house numbers and mounting hardware
- Exterior-grade screws, bolts, or nails
- Wood or metal post (if installing a new mailbox post)
- Concrete mix (if installing a new mailbox post)
- Exterior caulk or sealant (if necessary)

3. Removing the Old Mailbox and House Numbers:

Before installing the new components, remove the old mailbox and house numbers carefully to avoid damaging the surrounding surfaces.

a. Mailbox:

- If the mailbox is mounted on a post, remove any screws or bolts securing the mailbox to the post.
- If the mailbox is mounted on a wall or other surface, remove any screws, nails, or adhesive holding it in place.
- If the mailbox is in good condition, consider donating it or repurposing it for another use.

b. House Numbers:

- Carefully remove the old house numbers from the mounting surface, whether they are attached with screws, nails, or adhesive.

- If the numbers are difficult to remove, use a heat gun or hair dryer to soften any adhesive, or gently pry them off with a flathead screwdriver.
- Clean the mounting surface thoroughly to remove any residue or debris.

4. Installing the New Mailbox:

With the old mailbox removed, you can now install the new mailbox according to the manufacturer's instructions and local guidelines.

a. Mailbox Post (if applicable):
- If installing a new mailbox post, dig a hole approximately 2 feet deep and 6 inches wide.
- Place the post in the hole, ensuring it is level and plumb.
- Pour concrete mix into the hole, following the manufacturer's instructions for mixing and curing.
- Allow the concrete to set fully before proceeding with mailbox installation.

b. Mounting the Mailbox:
- If using a mailbox post, attach the mailbox to the post using the provided hardware or exterior-grade screws or bolts.
- If mounting the mailbox on a wall or other surface, use appropriate fasteners and anchors to secure it in place.
- Ensure the mailbox is level and securely attached to prevent it from falling or being easily knocked over.

5. Installing the New House Numbers:

After installing the mailbox, proceed with installing the new house numbers on your home's exterior.

a. Positioning the Numbers:
- Determine the best location for the house numbers, ensuring they are easily visible from the street and not obstructed by trees, shrubs, or other elements.
- Use a level to ensure the numbers are straight and evenly spaced.

161

- Mark the positions of the numbers with a pencil or tape before drilling or attaching them.

b. Attaching the Numbers:
- Depending on the type of numbers and mounting surface, use appropriate fasteners (e.g., screws, nails, or adhesive) to secure the numbers in place.
- Pre-drill holes for screws or nails if necessary to prevent cracking or splitting the mounting surface.
- Apply exterior caulk or sealant around the numbers if needed to prevent water infiltration and ensure a neat appearance.

6. Maintaining Your New Mailbox and House Numbers:

To keep your new mailbox and house numbers looking their best and functioning properly, perform regular maintenance and cleaning.

a. Mailbox:
- Periodically check the mailbox for signs of wear, damage, or rust, and address any issues promptly.
- Clean the mailbox regularly with a mild detergent and soft cloth to remove dirt, grime, and stains.
- Apply a coat of rust-resistant paint or sealant to metal mailboxes every few years to protect against the elements.

b. House Numbers:
- Clean the house numbers regularly with a mild detergent and soft cloth to maintain their visibility and appearance.
- Inspect the numbers periodically for any signs of damage, loosening, or fading, and replace or reattach them as needed.
- Trim any surrounding foliage or remove obstructions that may hinder the visibility of the numbers from the street.

By following these steps and selecting high-quality, durable materials, you can successfully replace your mailbox and house numbers, enhancing your home's curb appeal and ensuring proper mail delivery and visitor navigation. Remember to adhere to local guidelines and prioritize safety when working with tools and materials.

If you encounter any challenges or are unsure about any part of the replacement process, don't hesitate to consult a professional handyman or contractor for guidance or assistance. With a well-maintained mailbox and clearly visible house numbers, you can contribute to the overall appearance and functionality of your home's exterior.

Pressure Washing Exteriors

Pressure washing is an effective and efficient method for cleaning and maintaining the exterior surfaces of your home, including siding, driveways, decks, and patios. Using a high-pressure water spray, pressure washing removes dirt, grime, mildew, and other buildup, restoring the appearance and integrity of your home's exterior. In this section, we'll guide you through the process of pressure washing exteriors, including the steps for preparation, safety, cleaning, and maintenance.

1. Understanding Pressure Washing Equipment:

Before beginning the pressure washing process, it's essential to understand the equipment and its settings.

a. Pressure Washer Types:

- Electric pressure washers are suitable for light-duty tasks and are quieter and more compact than gas-powered models.
- Gas-powered pressure washers offer higher pressure and flow rates, making them better suited for heavy-duty cleaning and larger surfaces.

b. Nozzles and Attachments:

- Pressure washers come with interchangeable nozzles that control the water pressure and spray pattern.
- Use a wider nozzle (25-40 degrees) for general cleaning and a narrower nozzle (0-15 degrees) for tough stains or hard-to-reach areas.
- Some pressure washers have additional attachments, such as surface cleaners or brush attachments, for specific cleaning tasks.

2. Safety Precautions:

Pressure washing can be dangerous if not performed properly, so it's crucial to prioritize safety.

a. Personal Protective Equipment (PPE):

- Wear safety goggles to protect your eyes from debris and water spray.

- Use ear protection if operating a loud gas-powered pressure washer.
- Wear closed-toe shoes with good traction to prevent slips and falls.
- Consider wearing gloves to protect your hands from cleaning solutions and debris.

b. Electrical Safety:
- When using an electric pressure washer, ensure that all connections and extension cords are properly grounded and rated for outdoor use.
- Keep the pressure washer and electrical connections away from water and wet surfaces.

c. General Safety:
- Never point the pressure washer spray at people, animals, or electrical devices.
- Maintain a safe distance from the surface being cleaned to avoid damage or injury from debris.
- Use caution when working on ladders or elevated surfaces, ensuring stable footing and proper support.

3. Preparing the Area:

Before pressure washing, take steps to prepare the area and protect any sensitive surfaces or items.

a. Clearing the Area:
- Remove any furniture, potted plants, or décor from the surfaces to be cleaned.
- Cover or move any nearby items that could be damaged by water spray or debris.

b. Protecting Sensitive Surfaces:
- Use drop cloths or plastic sheeting to cover plants, landscaping, or other surfaces that could be damaged by cleaning solutions or high-pressure water.
- Tape plastic sheeting over electrical outlets, light fixtures, or vents to prevent water infiltration.

c. Pre-Cleaning:
- Sweep or brush away loose debris from the surfaces to be cleaned.
- Pre-treat heavily soiled or stained areas with a cleaning solution or degreaser, following the manufacturer's instructions.

4. Pressure Washing Techniques:
When pressure washing exteriors, use the appropriate techniques to achieve the best results and avoid damage.

a. Starting at a Distance:
- Begin pressure washing at a distance of about 4-5 feet from the surface, using a wide nozzle setting.
- Gradually move closer to the surface as needed, adjusting the nozzle for more focused cleaning.

b. Overlapping Strokes:
- Use overlapping strokes to ensure even coverage and avoid missing any spots.
- Work from top to bottom and from one side to the other for a systematic approach.

c. Maintaining Consistent Distance and Pressure:
- Keep the nozzle at a consistent distance from the surface to avoid creating streaks or damage.
- Maintain a steady pressure and move the nozzle at a consistent speed for even cleaning.

d. Rinsing and Drying:
- After pressure washing, use a wider nozzle setting to rinse the surface thoroughly, removing any remaining cleaning solution or debris.
- Allow the surface to air dry completely before replacing any furniture or décor.

5. Cleaning Solutions and Detergents:

While pressure washing alone can be effective, using cleaning solutions or detergents can help remove stubborn stains and improve results.

a. Choosing the Right Product:

- Select a cleaning solution or detergent that is appropriate for the surface material and type of stain or buildup.
- Consider eco-friendly or biodegradable options to minimize environmental impact.

b. Applying Cleaning Solutions:

- Apply the cleaning solution using a low-pressure setting or a separate sprayer attachment.
- Allow the solution to dwell on the surface for the recommended time before pressure washing.

c. Avoiding Damage:

- Test the cleaning solution on a small, inconspicuous area first to ensure it doesn't cause discoloration or damage.
- Follow the manufacturer's instructions for dilution ratios and application methods to prevent any adverse effects.

6. Maintaining Exterior Surfaces:

Regular pressure washing and maintenance can help extend the life and appearance of your home's exterior surfaces.

a. Frequency:

- Pressure wash your home's exterior annually or as needed, depending on the level of buildup and environmental factors.
- High-humidity or heavily wooded areas may require more frequent cleaning to prevent mildew or algae growth.

b. Preventive Measures:

- Trim nearby trees or foliage to reduce the amount of debris and shade on exterior surfaces.
- Ensure proper drainage around your home to prevent water from pooling and contributing to mildew or stain formation.

c. Addressing Damage:
- Inspect exterior surfaces regularly for signs of damage, such as cracks, gaps, or peeling paint.
- Repair any damage promptly to prevent further deterioration and maintain the integrity of your home's exterior.

By following these steps and using the appropriate equipment and techniques, you can effectively pressure wash your home's exterior surfaces, improving their appearance and protecting them from damage. Remember to prioritize safety, use the right cleaning solutions, and maintain a consistent cleaning schedule to keep your home looking its best.

If you encounter any challenges or are unsure about any part of the pressure washing process, consider consulting a professional pressure washing service for guidance or assistance. With regular pressure washing and maintenance, you can enhance your home's curb appeal and extend the life of its exterior surfaces.

Chapter 8
Energy-Efficient Upgrades
Installing a Programmable Thermostat

Installing a programmable thermostat is an effective way to improve your home's energy efficiency, reduce your utility bills, and enhance your comfort. A programmable thermostat allows you to automatically adjust your home's temperature settings based on your daily schedule and preferences, minimizing energy waste and ensuring optimal comfort when you need it most. In this section, we'll guide you through the process of installing a programmable thermostat, including the steps for selecting the right model, preparing for installation, wiring, and programming.

1. Choosing the Right Programmable Thermostat:
   Before beginning the installation process, select a programmable thermostat that suits your heating and cooling system and meets your needs.
   a. Compatibility:
   • Determine the type of heating and cooling system you have (e.g., single-stage, multi-stage, or heat pump) to ensure compatibility with the thermostat.
   • Check the voltage requirements of your system (usually 24 V or 120/240V) and choose a thermostat that matches.
   b. Features:
   • Consider the features you want in a programmable thermostat, such as touchscreen displays, Wi-Fi connectivity, or remote access via smartphone apps.
   • Look for models with easy-to-use interfaces and clear instructions for programming.
   c. Energy Efficiency:
   • Choose a programmable thermostat that is ENERGY STAR certified, indicating that it meets strict energy efficiency guidelines.

- Some models offer adaptive recovery or learning features that optimize your system's performance based on your habits and preferences.

2. Preparing for Installation:

Before installing your new programmable thermostat, take the necessary steps to ensure a safe and successful installation.

a. Safety Precautions:
- Turn off the power to your heating and cooling system at the circuit breaker or fuse box to prevent electrical shock.
- Verify that the power is off using a non-contact voltage tester on the existing thermostat wires.

b. Removing the Old Thermostat:
- Remove the old thermostat's cover and take a picture of the existing wiring for reference.
- Label each wire with the corresponding terminal letter using adhesive labels or masking tape.
- Disconnect the wires from the old thermostat and carefully remove it from the wall.

c. Preparing the Wall:
- Patch any holes or damage to the wall surface where the old thermostat was mounted.
- If necessary, use a drywall saw to create a new hole for the programmable thermostat's mounting plate.

3. Wiring the Programmable Thermostat:

With the old thermostat removed and the wall prepared, you can now wire the new programmable thermostat according to the manufacturer's instructions.

a. Mounting the Thermostat:
- Secure the new thermostat's mounting plate to the wall using the provided screws and anchors.
- Pull the labeled wires through the opening in the mounting plate.

b. Connecting the Wires:
- Refer to the wiring diagram provided with your programmable thermostat and the picture of your old thermostat's wiring.
- Match the labeled wires to the corresponding terminals on the new thermostat and securely attach them, following the manufacturer's instructions.
- If you have any unused wires, cap them off with wire nuts to prevent them from touching other terminals.

c. Installing Batteries (if applicable):
- Some programmable thermostats require batteries for backup power during outages.
- Install fresh batteries according to the manufacturer's instructions, ensuring proper polarity.

4. Programming the Thermostat:

Once the programmable thermostat is wired and mounted, you can now set up your temperature schedules and preferences.

a. Initial Setup:
- Turn the power back on to your heating and cooling system at the circuit breaker or fuse box.
- Follow the manufacturer's instructions for initial setup, which may include setting the date, time, and system type.

b. Creating Temperature Schedules:
- Most programmable thermostats allow you to set different temperature schedules for weekdays and weekends.
- Divide your day into periods (e.g., wake, leave, return, sleep) and assign your desired temperature setpoints for each period.
- Consider your family's daily routines and adjust the schedules accordingly to optimize comfort and energy savings.

c. Setting Hold Temperatures:
- Set your desired hold temperatures for when you're away on vacation or during extended periods of consistent temperature needs.

- Many programmable thermostats offer a "vacation" or "hold" mode that maintains a constant temperature until you return to your regular schedule.

5. Testing and Adjusting:
After programming your thermostat, test its operation to ensure it's controlling your heating and cooling system properly.
a. System Test:
- Adjust the temperature setpoint to initiate heating or cooling and verify that your system responds accordingly.
- Listen for the sound of your system turning on and feel for air flow from your vents to confirm proper operation.

b. Fine-Tuning Schedules:
- Over the next few days, monitor your home's temperature and comfort levels during each programmed period.
- Make adjustments to your temperature setpoints and schedules as needed to achieve the desired balance of comfort and energy efficiency.

6. Maintaining Your Programmable Thermostat:
To ensure optimal performance and energy savings, maintain your programmable thermostat with regular care and updates.
a. Battery Replacement:
- If your thermostat uses batteries, replace them annually or as indicated by a low battery warning.
- Use high-quality, fresh batteries to prevent any disruptions in operation.
b. Seasonal Adjustments:
- Review and adjust your temperature schedules at the beginning of each heating and cooling season to account for changing weather conditions and comfort preferences.
- Consider setting your thermostat to "auto" mode to allow it to switch between heating and cooling as needed during transitional seasons.

c. Software Updates:

- If your programmable thermostat has Wi-Fi connectivity, periodically check for software updates that may improve performance, security, or add new features.
- Follow the manufacturer's instructions for downloading and installing any available updates.

By following these steps and carefully programming your thermostat to match your lifestyle and comfort needs, you can maximize the energy efficiency and cost savings potential of your heating and cooling system. Remember to consult the manufacturer's instructions for specific guidance on wiring, programming, and troubleshooting.

If you encounter any challenges or are unsure about any part of the installation process, consider hiring a professional HVAC technician or electrician for assistance. With a properly installed and programmed thermostat, you can enjoy improved comfort, convenience, and energy efficiency in your home for years to come.

Weatherstripping Doors and Windows

Weatherstripping is an essential home maintenance task that involves sealing the gaps around doors and windows to prevent drafts, improve energy efficiency, and increase comfort. By reducing air leaks, weatherstripping helps maintain a consistent indoor temperature, reduces strain on your heating and cooling system, and ultimately saves you money on energy bills. In this section, we'll guide you through the process of weatherstripping doors and windows, including the steps for selecting materials, preparing surfaces, and installing various types of weatherstripping.

1. Identifying Air Leaks:

Before beginning the weatherstripping process, identify the areas around your doors and windows that require sealing.

a. Visual Inspection:

- Check for visible gaps, cracks, or daylight showing around the edges of doors and windows.
- Look for signs of wear, damage, or deterioration on existing weatherstripping.

b. Draft Detection:

- On a windy day, hold a lit candle or incense stick near the edges of doors and windows to detect air movement.
- If the flame or smoke wavers or is blown out, there is likely an air leak that needs to be sealed.

c. Professional Energy Audit:

- Consider hiring a professional energy auditor to perform a thorough assessment of your home's air leaks and provide recommendations for weatherstripping and other energy-saving measures.

2. Choosing Weatherstripping Materials:

There are several types of weatherstripping materials available, each with its own advantages and best uses.

a. Foam Tape:

- Foam tape is an affordable and easy-to-install option, suitable for sealing small gaps and irregular surfaces.
- It comes in various thicknesses and widths and has an adhesive backing for simple application.

b. Felt Strips:

- Felt strips are another economical choice, best used for sealing gaps between a door or window and its frame.
- They compress easily and are available in different thicknesses and colors.

c. Vinyl or Silicone Bulb Seals:

- These flexible seals are ideal for gaps between a door and its threshold or a window and its sill.
- They are durable, resistant to moisture and temperature changes, and come in various colors to match your door or window.

d. Metal Weatherstripping:

- Metal weatherstripping, such as bronze or stainless steel, is a long-lasting and sturdy option for sealing larger gaps.
- It is often used on the bottom of doors or in commercial settings and requires professional installation.

3. Preparing Surfaces:

Before installing weatherstripping, clean and prepare the surfaces around your doors and windows to ensure proper adhesion and effectiveness.

a. Cleaning:

- Remove any old weatherstripping, adhesive residue, or debris from the door or window frame.
- Clean the surfaces thoroughly with soap and water, then allow them to dry completely.

b. Sanding (if necessary):

- If the surfaces are rough or uneven, use fine-grit sandpaper to create a smooth surface for the weatherstripping to adhere to.
- Wipe away any sanding dust with a clean, dry cloth.

c. Measuring and Cutting:

- Measure the length of each side of the door or window frame where weatherstripping will be applied.
- Cut the weatherstripping material to the appropriate lengths, allowing for a slight overlap at the corners for a tight seal.

4. Installing Weatherstripping:

The installation process may vary slightly depending on the type of weatherstripping material you have chosen.

a. Foam Tape:

- Peel off the adhesive backing and apply the foam tape to the clean, dry surface, pressing firmly to ensure good contact.
- For doors, apply the tape to the doorstop (the frame where the door rests when closed) on the top and sides.
- For windows, apply the tape to the sash (the movable part of the window) or the frame, depending on where the gap is located.

b. Felt Strips:

- Nail or staple the felt strips along the door or window frame, ensuring they compress slightly when the door or window is closed.
- For doors, attach the strips to the doorstop on the top and sides, and to the threshold at the bottom.
- For windows, attach the strips to the sash or frame, depending on the location of the gap.

c. Vinyl or Silicone Bulb Seals:

- For doors, attach the bulb seal to the threshold using the provided screws or adhesive, ensuring that the seal compresses when the door closes.

- For windows, attach the bulb seal to the sash or frame where the gap is located, using the provided adhesive or screws.

d. Metal Weatherstripping:
- Due to the complexity of installation, it is recommended to hire a professional to install metal weatherstripping.
- They will cut the weatherstripping to size, form it to fit the contours of your door or window, and secure it in place using screws or nails.

5. Testing and Adjusting:

After installing the weatherstripping, test its effectiveness and make any necessary adjustments.

a. Closing and Opening:
- Close and open the door or window several times to ensure that the weatherstripping does not interfere with its operation.
- Check that the door or window seals properly and that there are no gaps or air leaks.

b. Adjusting:
- If you notice any gaps or if the door or window is difficult to open or close, adjust the weatherstripping placement or compression until a proper seal is achieved.
- Trim any excess weatherstripping material that may be impeding the door or window's movement.

6. Maintaining Weatherstripping:

To ensure the long-term effectiveness of your weatherstripping, perform regular maintenance and inspections.

a. Cleaning:
- Periodically clean the weatherstripping with a damp cloth to remove dust, dirt, and debris that can compromise the seal.
- Avoid using harsh chemicals or abrasive cleaners that may damage the weatherstripping material.

b. Inspection:

- Annually inspect the weatherstripping for signs of wear, damage, or gaps.
- Check that the weatherstripping remains securely attached and properly compressed when the door or window is closed.

c. Replacement:

- If the weatherstripping becomes worn, damaged, or loses its effectiveness, replace it promptly to maintain a tight seal and optimal energy efficiency.
- Remove the old weatherstripping and install new material following the same steps as the initial installation.

By following these steps and maintaining your weatherstripping regularly, you can significantly improve your home's energy efficiency, comfort, and indoor air quality. Weatherstripping is a cost-effective way to reduce drafts, minimize energy waste, and create a more pleasant living environment.

If you encounter any challenges or are unsure about the best weatherstripping solution for your specific doors and windows, consult with a home improvement professional or energy efficiency expert for guidance. With properly installed and maintained weatherstripping, you can enjoy a more comfortable and energy-efficient home for years to come.

Insulating an Attic and Crawl Space

Proper insulation in your attic and crawl space is crucial for maintaining a comfortable indoor temperature, reducing energy costs, and preventing moisture-related issues. Insulation acts as a barrier, slowing the transfer of heat between your living spaces and the unconditioned areas of your home. In this section, we'll guide you through the process of insulating an attic and crawl space, including the steps for choosing insulation materials, preparing the spaces, and installing the insulation effectively.

1. Assessing Insulation Needs:

Before beginning the insulation process, assess your current insulation levels and determine the appropriate amount of insulation needed for your climate and home.

a. Recommended R-Values:

- Consult local building codes and energy efficiency guidelines to determine the recommended insulation R-values for your attic and crawl space based on your climate zone.
- R-value measures the insulation's resistance to heat flow; higher R-values indicate better insulating properties.

b. Existing Insulation:

- Inspect your attic and crawl space to determine the type and depth of any existing insulation.
- If the insulation is damaged, compressed, or insufficient, it may need to be replaced or supplemented.

c. Ventilation:

- Ensure that your attic and crawl space have proper ventilation to prevent moisture buildup and maintain air quality.
- Check for and address any blocked vents, damaged vent screens, or inadequate ventilation before installing new insulation.

2. Choosing Insulation Materials:

There are several types of insulation materials available, each with its own advantages and best uses.

a. Fiberglass Batts:

- Fiberglass batts are pre-cut sections of insulation made from glass fibers and are a common choice for attics and crawl spaces.
- They are relatively inexpensive, easy to install, and available in various thicknesses and R-values.

b. Cellulose:

- Cellulose insulation is made from recycled paper products treated with fire retardants and is well-suited for attics and hard-to-reach areas.
- It can be blown in using special equipment, providing excellent coverage and air sealing.

c. Spray Foam:

- Spray foam insulation is a liquid that expands and hardens when applied, creating an air-tight seal and high insulating value.
- It is more expensive than other options but offers superior energy efficiency and moisture control.

d. Rigid Foam Board:

- Rigid foam board insulation is made from polystyrene or polyisocyanurate and is an excellent choice for insulating crawl space walls.
- It has a high R-value per inch of thickness and can be cut to fit around obstacles and utilities.

3. Preparing the Space:

Before installing insulation, prepare your attic and crawl space to ensure a safe and effective installation process.

a. Clearing the Area:

- Remove any stored items, debris, or obstructions from the attic and crawl space to provide clear access for insulation installation.

- Repair any damaged or rotted framing, and replace any missing or damaged insulation before proceeding.

b. Air Sealing:
- Identify and seal any air leaks in the attic and crawl space, such as gaps around pipes, wires, or ducts, using expandable foam or caulk.
- Pay special attention to the areas where walls meet the attic floor and where the foundation meets the crawl space walls.

c. Vapor Barrier (Crawl Space):
- If your crawl space has a dirt floor, install a vapor barrier (6-mil polyethylene sheeting) to cover the ground and prevent moisture from seeping into the insulation.
- Overlap the seams of the vapor barrier by at least 6 inches and secure it to the walls with tape or mechanical fasteners.

4. Installing Attic Insulation:

The installation process for attic insulation will depend on the type of insulation material you have chosen.

a. Fiberglass Batts:
- Start by insulating the attic floor, placing the batts between the joists and ensuring they fit snugly without compression.
- If there is existing insulation, place the new batts on top, perpendicular to the old ones to cover the joists and prevent heat bridging.
- Use a utility knife to cut the batts as needed to fit around obstacles and maintain a consistent depth.

b. Cellulose:
- Rent or hire a professional to use a blowing machine to install cellulose insulation in your attic.
- Begin at the furthest corner from the attic access and work your way back, applying an even layer of insulation to the desired depth.
- Take care not to block any vents or air channels, and maintain a 3-inch clearance around recessed lighting fixtures and flues.

c. Spray Foam:
- Due to the complexity and specialized equipment required, it is recommended to hire a professional insulation contractor to install spray foam insulation.
- They will ensure proper application depth, air sealing, and ventilation to maximize energy efficiency and prevent moisture issues.

5. Installing Crawl Space Insulation:

Insulating a crawl space involves sealing and insulating the walls rather than the floor above.

a. Rigid Foam Board:
- Measure and cut the rigid foam board to fit the height of the crawl space walls, allowing for a 2-inch gap at the top for air circulation.
- Secure the foam board to the walls using mechanical fasteners or adhesive, ensuring a snug fit between pieces.
- Seal any seams or gaps between the boards with foam-compatible tape or caulk to prevent air leaks.

b. Fiberglass Batts:
- If using fiberglass batts, install them in the rim joist area (where the foundation meets the floor joists) for added insulation.
- Cut the batts to fit snugly in the space, and use a staple gun or insulation supports to hold them in place.

c. Spray Foam:
- If opting for spray foam insulation, hire a professional contractor to apply it to the crawl space walls and rim joist area.
- They will ensure proper thickness, air sealing, and ventilation to create a moisture-resistant and energy-efficient crawl space.

6. Post-Installation Considerations:

After installing insulation in your attic and crawl space, take steps to ensure its long-term effectiveness and safety.

a. Attic Ventilation:

- Ensure that your attic has adequate ventilation to prevent heat and moisture buildup, which can damage insulation and lead to mold growth.
- Install or maintain soffit vents, ridge vents, or gable vents as needed to promote proper air circulation.

b. Crawl Space Monitoring:

- Regularly inspect your crawl space for signs of moisture, pests, or insulation damage.
- Address any issues promptly to maintain a healthy and energy-efficient home.

c. Safety:

- When working with insulation, wear appropriate personal protective equipment, such as gloves, a long-sleeved shirt, pants, and a dust mask or respirator.
- Follow the manufacturer's instructions and local building codes for installation and safety guidelines.

By following these steps and properly insulating your attic and crawl space, you can significantly improve your home's energy efficiency, comfort, and indoor air quality. Insulation is a cost-effective way to reduce heat loss in winter, keep your home cooler in summer, and prevent moisture-related issues in unconditioned spaces.

If you encounter any challenges or are unsure about the best insulation solution for your specific home, consult with a home energy professional or insulation contractor for guidance. With well-installed and maintained insulation in your attic and crawl space, you can enjoy a more comfortable and energy-efficient home while also protecting your home's structural integrity.

Replacing Old Appliances with Energy-Efficient Models

Replacing old, inefficient appliances with energy-efficient models is an excellent way to reduce your home's energy consumption, lower your utility bills, and minimize your environmental impact. Energy-efficient appliances use advanced technologies and design features to deliver superior performance while using less electricity or natural gas. In this section, we'll guide you through the process of replacing old appliances with energy-efficient models, including the steps for assessing your current appliances, choosing the right replacements, and ensuring proper installation and maintenance.

1. Assessing Your Current Appliances:
   Before replacing your appliances, assess their energy efficiency and determine which ones are the best candidates for replacement.
   a. Age and Condition:
   • Consider the age and overall condition of your current appliances. Appliances over 10-15 years old are likely to be less energy-efficient than newer models.
   • Look for signs of wear, damage, or poor performance, such as inconsistent temperatures in refrigerators or long drying times for clothes dryers.
   b. Energy Consumption:
   • Check the energy labels on your current appliances to determine their annual energy consumption and compare it to newer, energy-efficient models.
   • Use online tools or consult with an energy professional to estimate the potential energy and cost savings of replacing specific appliances.
   c. Repair vs. Replace:
   • If an appliance is relatively new and in good condition, it may be more cost-effective to repair it rather than replace it.

- However, if an appliance is old, inefficient, and requires frequent or expensive repairs, replacement with an energy-efficient model is often the better long-term solution.

2. Choosing Energy-Efficient Appliances:
When selecting new appliances, look for models that offer the best combination of energy efficiency, performance, and features for your needs and budget.
a. ENERGY STAR Label:
- Choose appliances that bear the ENERGY STAR label, which signifies that they meet strict energy efficiency guidelines set by the U.S. Environmental Protection Agency (EPA).
- ENERGY STAR certified appliances often use 10-50% less energy than standard models, depending on the appliance type and size.
b. Energy Guide Label:
- Review the Energy Guide label on prospective appliances to compare their annual energy consumption and estimated operating costs.
- The label also shows the appliance's energy use relative to similar models, helping you identify the most efficient options within a particular category.
c. Size and Capacity:
- Select appliances that are appropriately sized for your household's needs to avoid wasting energy on unused capacity.
- Consider factors such as your family size, lifestyle, and usage patterns when choosing appliance sizes and features.

3. Installing and Setting Up Energy-Efficient Appliances:
Proper installation and setup are crucial for ensuring that your new energy-efficient appliances perform optimally and deliver the expected energy savings.

a. Professional Installation:

- Hire a qualified appliance installer or contractor to ensure that your new appliances are properly connected, leveled, and calibrated.
- Improper installation can lead to reduced efficiency, decreased performance, and even safety hazards.

b. Placement and Ventilation:

- Position your appliances in locations that promote efficient operation and adequate ventilation.
- For example, avoid placing refrigerators or freezers in direct sunlight or near heat sources, and ensure that air can circulate freely around the condenser coils.

c. Initial Settings and Calibration:

- Adjust the initial settings on your new appliances to optimize their energy efficiency and performance.
- Set refrigerator and freezer temperatures to the recommended levels, typically 35-38°F (1.7-3.3°C) for the fresh food compartment and 0°F (-17.8°C) for the freezer.
- For washers, dryers, and dishwashers, select the appropriate cycle settings and water temperatures for your typical loads and soil levels.

4. Using Energy-Efficient Appliances Efficiently:

In addition to choosing energy-efficient appliances, it's important to use them in ways that maximize their efficiency and minimize waste.

a. Full Loads:

- Run your dishwasher, washing machine, and dryer with full loads whenever possible to make the most of each cycle's energy consumption.
- Avoid overloading appliances, as this can reduce efficiency and lead to suboptimal cleaning or drying results.

b. Temperature Settings:
- Adjust temperature settings on your refrigerator, freezer, and water heater to the most efficient levels that still meet your needs.
- For clothes washing, use cold water whenever possible, as heating water accounts for a significant portion of a washing machine's energy use.

c. Maintenance and Cleaning:
- Regularly clean and maintain your appliances to ensure they continue to operate at peak efficiency.
- For example, clean your refrigerator's condenser coils, replace your dishwasher's filters, and clean your washing machine's lint trap after each use.

5. Recycling Old Appliances:

When replacing old appliances, be sure to dispose of them responsibly to minimize their environmental impact and potentially earn rebates or incentives.

a. Recycling Programs:
- Many utilities, municipalities, and appliance retailers offer recycling programs for old appliances, often with free pickup and disposal services.
- Recycling ensures that the materials in your old appliances are recovered and reused, reducing waste and conserving resources.

b. Rebates and Incentives:
- Some utilities and local governments offer rebates or incentives for recycling old appliances when you purchase new, energy-efficient models.
- Check with your local utility or visit the ENERGY STAR Rebate Finder website to identify available rebates and incentives in your area.

6. Monitoring and Adjusting Energy Use:

After replacing your old appliances with energy-efficient models, continue to monitor your home's energy consumption and make adjustments as needed to maximize savings.

a. Energy Monitoring:

- Use your utility bills or a home energy monitor to track your energy consumption over time and identify any unusual spikes or patterns.
- Compare your energy use before and after replacing appliances to gauge the impact of your upgrades.

b. Behavioral Changes:

- Adopt energy-saving habits and practices to further reduce your appliance-related energy consumption.
- For example, turn off and unplug appliances when not in use, use natural drying methods for clothes when possible, and minimize the time your refrigerator or freezer door remains open.

c. Continuous Improvement:

- As your appliances age or your household needs change, reassess their energy efficiency and consider additional upgrades or replacements as warranted.
- Stay informed about the latest advancements in appliance technology and energy efficiency standards to make informed decisions about future purchases.

By following these steps and making smart choices when replacing old appliances with energy-efficient models, you can significantly reduce your home's energy consumption, save money on your utility bills, and contribute to a more sustainable future. While the upfront costs of purchasing energy-efficient appliances may be higher than those of standard models, the long-term energy savings and environmental benefits make them a wise investment for most homeowners.

If you need assistance or guidance in selecting the best energy-efficient appliances for your home, consult with a home energy professional, appliance specialist, or your local utility's energy efficiency program. They can provide personalized recommendations based on your specific needs, budget, and energy-saving goals. By making informed decisions and adopting energy-efficient practices, you can enjoy the many benefits of a more sustainable and cost-effective home.

Installing Low-Flow Showerheads and Faucets

Installing low-flow showerheads and faucets is an effective way to reduce your home's water consumption without sacrificing comfort or performance. Low-flow fixtures use advanced designs and technologies to deliver a satisfying flow rate while using significantly less water than standard models. By upgrading to low-flow showerheads and faucets, you can save water, reduce your energy costs for water heating, and contribute to the conservation of a precious natural resource. In this section, we'll guide you through the process of installing low-flow showerheads and faucets, including the steps for selecting the right fixtures, preparing for installation, and ensuring proper function and maintenance.

1. Understanding Low-Flow Fixtures:

Before selecting low-flow showerheads and faucets, it's important to understand how they differ from standard fixtures and the benefits they offer.

a. Flow Rates:
- Low-flow showerheads typically have a maximum flow rate of 2.0 gallons per minute (GPM) or less, compared to standard showerheads that can use 2.5 GPM or more.
- Low-flow faucets generally have a maximum flow rate of 1.5 GPM or less, while standard faucets can use 2.2 GPM or more.

b. Water Savings:
- By reducing the flow rate, low-flow fixtures can significantly reduce your water consumption without noticeably affecting the user experience.
- Over time, these water savings can add up to substantial reductions in your water bills and your home's overall environmental impact.

c. Energy Savings:
- Because low-flow fixtures use less water, they also require less energy to heat that water, resulting in energy savings and lower utility bills.
- This is especially beneficial for showers, as showering accounts for a significant portion of a household's hot water use.

2. Choosing Low-Flow Showerheads and Faucets:
When selecting low-flow fixtures, consider factors such as flow rate, design, and compatibility with your existing plumbing.
a. WaterSense Label:
- Look for showerheads and faucets that bear the WaterSense label, which indicates that they meet the EPA's stringent criteria for water efficiency and performance.
- WaterSense-labeled fixtures are independently certified to use at least 20% less water than standard models while delivering equal or superior performance.
b. Flow Rate and Design:
- Choose low-flow showerheads and faucets with flow rates that meet your preferences and needs. Some models offer adjustable flow settings for added flexibility.
- Consider the design and finish of the fixtures to ensure they complement your bathroom or kitchen décor and provide the desired functionality.
c. Compatibility:
- Ensure that the low-flow fixtures you select are compatible with your existing plumbing and water pressure.
- Some low-flow models may require a minimum water pressure to function properly, so check your home's water pressure and consult with a plumbing professional if needed.

3. Preparing for Installation:

Before installing your low-flow showerheads and faucets, gather the necessary tools and materials and prepare your work area.

a. Tools and Materials:
- Adjustable wrench or pliers
- Teflon tape (plumber's tape)
- Cloth or towel
- Bucket
- Replacement washers or O-rings (if needed)

b. Turning Off Water Supply:
- Locate the main water shut-off valve for your home and turn it off to prevent any water from flowing during the installation process.
- If your home has separate shut-off valves for each fixture, you may turn off only the relevant valves for the showerhead or faucet you're replacing.

c. Removing Old Fixtures:
- Use an adjustable wrench or pliers to carefully remove the old showerhead or faucet, taking care not to damage the plumbing or wall surfaces.
- If the old fixture is difficult to remove, apply penetrating oil to the threads and allow it to sit for a few minutes before attempting to loosen it again.

4. Installing Low-Flow Showerheads:

Follow these steps to install your new low-flow showerhead:

a. Clean Threads:
- Clean the threads on the shower arm (the pipe coming out of the wall) to remove any old tape, debris, or mineral buildup.
- Use a cloth or an old toothbrush to ensure the threads are clean and free of any obstructions.

b. Apply Teflon Tape:
- Wrap Teflon tape clockwise around the threads of the shower arm, making sure to cover the threads completely.

- The Teflon tape helps to create a watertight seal and prevents leaks.

c. Attach Showerhead:
- Screw the new low-flow showerhead onto the shower arm by hand, ensuring a snug fit.
- Use an adjustable wrench or pliers to gently tighten the showerhead, being careful not to overtighten, as this can damage the threads or cause leaks.

5. Installing Low-Flow Faucets:

The process for installing low-flow faucets is similar to that of showerheads, with a few additional considerations:

a. Remove Aerator:
- Before installing the new faucet, remove the aerator (the small screen at the tip of the faucet) and clean any debris or mineral buildup.
- If the new faucet comes with a new aerator, you may discard the old one.

b. Replace Washers or O-Rings:
- If your new faucet includes replacement washers or O-rings, install them according to the manufacturer's instructions to ensure a proper seal and prevent leaks.

c. Attach Faucet:
- Connect the new low-flow faucet to the water supply lines, ensuring a snug fit and using Teflon tape on the threads if recommended by the manufacturer.
- Use an adjustable wrench or pliers to gently tighten the connections, being careful not to overtighten and damage the fittings.

6. Testing and Adjusting:

After installing your low-flow showerheads and faucets, test them to ensure proper function and make any necessary adjustments.

a. Turn On Water Supply:

- Turn the main water shut-off valve (or individual fixture valves) back on slowly, checking for any leaks or drips around the connections.
- If leaks are present, turn the water off and gently tighten the connections or apply additional Teflon tape as needed.

b. Test Flow and Temperature:

- Turn on your new low-flow showerhead or faucet and check the flow rate and water temperature.
- Adjust the fixture's settings (if applicable) to achieve your desired flow and temperature, following the manufacturer's instructions.

c. Fine-Tune and Troubleshoot:

- If the flow seems too low or the water pressure is inconsistent, check for any obstructions in the aerator or showerhead and clean as necessary.
- Consult the manufacturer's troubleshooting guide or contact a plumbing professional if you encounter any persistent issues or leaks.

7. Maintenance and Conservation Tips:

To ensure the longevity and efficiency of your low-flow fixtures, follow these maintenance and conservation tips:

a. Regular Cleaning:

- Clean your low-flow showerheads and faucets regularly to prevent mineral buildup and maintain optimal performance.
- Soak the fixtures in a solution of equal parts white vinegar and water for several hours, then scrub gently with a soft brush or cloth to remove any deposits.

b. Leak Detection and Repair:
- Periodically check for any leaks or drips around your low-flow fixtures and promptly repair them to avoid water waste and potential damage.
- A slow drip from a showerhead or faucet can waste a significant amount of water over time, undermining the savings from your low-flow fixtures.

c. Water-Saving Habits:
- In addition to installing low-flow fixtures, adopt water-saving habits to further reduce your consumption, such as taking shorter showers, turning off the tap while brushing your teeth, and fixing any leaky toilets or pipes.
- Encourage all household members to be mindful of their water use and to look for ways to conserve this valuable resource.

By following these steps and maintaining your low-flow showerheads and faucets properly, you can enjoy significant water and energy savings without sacrificing comfort or convenience. While the installation process may seem daunting at first, most homeowners can successfully complete this project with basic tools and a little patience.

If you encounter any challenges or are unsure about your ability to install low-flow fixtures safely, don't hesitate to consult with a licensed plumber or a home improvement professional. They can provide expert guidance and ensure that your new fixtures are installed correctly and in compliance with local building codes.

By making the switch to low-flow showerheads and faucets, you'll be taking an important step toward a more sustainable and environmentally responsible home while also saving money on your utility bills. As more homeowners adopt water-efficient practices and technologies, we can collectively reduce our impact on the planet's limited freshwater resources and help to ensure a more secure water future for generations to come.

Conclusion

Congratulations on making it to the end of this comprehensive guide on DIY home improvement projects! By now, you should feel empowered and equipped with the knowledge and skills needed to tackle a wide range of projects around your home, from basic repairs and maintenance to more advanced renovations and upgrades.

Throughout this book, we've covered a diverse array of topics, including essential tools and techniques, plumbing and electrical work, flooring and wall coverings, outdoor improvements, and energy-efficient upgrades. Each section has been carefully crafted to provide you with detailed, step-by-step instructions, practical tips, and safety guidelines to ensure your success and confidence as a DIY enthusiast.

Remember, the key to successful home improvement projects lies in proper planning, preparation, and execution. Always take the time to assess your skills, gather the necessary tools and materials, and follow instructions carefully. Don't hesitate to seek guidance from professionals or experienced friends and family members when needed, and prioritize safety above all else.

As you embark on your DIY journey, embrace the challenges and learning opportunities that come with each project. Celebrate your successes, no matter how small, and learn from any setbacks or mistakes. With practice and perseverance, you'll develop a keen eye for detail, a problem-solving mindset, and a deep sense of pride in your home and your abilities.

In addition to the practical benefits of DIY home improvement, such as saving money and increasing your home's value, these projects also offer a unique opportunity for personal growth and fulfillment.

As you transform your living space, you'll also be nurturing your creativity, resilience, and self-reliance - valuable qualities that extend far beyond the walls of your home.

So, whether you're a seasoned DIY veteran or a curious beginner, keep this guide close at hand as a trusted reference and source of inspiration. Share your knowledge and experiences with others, and continue to explore the vast world of home improvement. With each project you undertake, you'll be not only enhancing your home but also building a legacy of craftsmanship, ingenuity, and pride that will last for years to come.

Here's to your future DIY successes and the joy of creating a home that truly reflects your style, values, and dreams!

Made in the USA
Columbia, SC
21 June 2025

59694184R00109